Overcoming ADHD
in Adolescence

 PROGRAMS THAT WORK

✔ PROGRAMS THAT WORK

Overcoming ADHD in Adolescence

A Cognitive Behavioral Approach

CLIENT WORKBOOK

SUSAN E. SPRICH

STEVEN A. SAFREN

OXFORD
UNIVERSITY PRESS

OXFORD
UNIVERSITY PRESS

Oxford University Press is a department of the University of Oxford. It furthers
the University's objective of excellence in research, scholarship, and education
by publishing worldwide. Oxford is a registered trade mark of Oxford University
Press in the UK and certain other countries.

Published in the United States of America by Oxford University Press
198 Madison Avenue, New York, NY 10016, United States of America.

Library of Congress Cataloging-in-Publication Data
Names: Sprich, Susan E., author. | Safren, Steven A., author.
Title: Overcoming ADHD in adolescence : a cognitive behavioral approach -
client workbook / Susan E. Sprich, Steven A. Safren.
Description: New York : Oxford University Press, [2020] |
Series: Programs that work |
Includes bibliographical references and index.
Identifiers: LCCN 2019053111 (print) | LCCN 2019053112 (ebook) |
ISBN 9780190854485 (paperback) | ISBN 9780190854508 (epub) |
ISBN 9780190854515
Subjects: LCSH: Attention-deficit disorder in adolescence. | Cognitive therapy.
Classification: LCC RJ506.H9 S6638 2020 (print) | LCC RJ506.H9 (ebook) |
DDC 616.85/8900835—dc23
LC record available at https://lccn.loc.gov/2019053111
LC ebook record available at https://lccn.loc.gov/2019053112

9 8 7 6 5 4 3 2 1

Printed by Marquis, Canada

One of the most difficult problems confronting patients with various disorders and diseases is finding the best help available. Everyone is aware of friends or family who have sought treatment from a seemingly reputable practitioner only to find out later from another doctor that the original diagnosis was wrong or the treatments recommended were inappropriate or perhaps even harmful. Most patients or family members address this problem by reading everything they can about their symptoms, seeking out information on the Internet, or aggressively "asking around" to tap knowledge from friends and acquaintances. Governments and healthcare policymakers are also aware that people in need don't always get the best treatments—something they refer to as "variability in healthcare practices."

Now healthcare systems around the world are attempting to correct this variability by introducing *evidence-based practice*. This simply means that it is in everyone's interest that patients get the most up-to-date and effective care for a particular problem. Healthcare policymakers have also recognized that it is very useful to give consumers of healthcare as much information as possible so that they can make intelligent decisions in a collaborative effort to improve health and mental health. This series, Programs *That Work*, is designed to accomplish just that. Only the latest and most effective interventions for particular problems are described in user-friendly language. To be included in this series, each treatment program must pass the highest standards of evidence available, as determined by a scientific advisory board. Thus, when individuals suffering from these problems or their family members seek out an expert clinician who is familiar with these interventions and decides that they are appropriate, they will have confidence that they are receiving the best care available. Of course, only your healthcare professional can decide on the right mix of treatments for you.

This attention-deficit/hyperactivity disorder (ADHD) workbook for adolescents will enable young people to build organizational and planning skills, reduce distractibility, and build adaptive thinking—all with the aim of helping young people struggling with ADHD to gain and maintain independence. Though the workbook is aimed at adolescents themselves, parents may also find it useful, particularly the concluding discussion on maintaining gains made in treatment. The workbook also features information on the use of technology to support treatment, as well as numerous forms and worksheets to aid in solidifying skills. This intervention is based on a rigorous program of research demonstrating its effectiveness and was designed and tested by two leading authorities in the science of ADHD treatment.

Anne Marie Albano, Editor-in-Chief
David H. Barlow, Editor-in-Chief
Programs *ThatWork*

Accessing Treatments *ThatWork* Forms and Worksheets Online

All forms and worksheets from books in the PTW series are made available digitally shortly following print publication. You may download, print, save, and digitally complete them as PDFs. To access the forms and worksheets, please visit http://www.oup.com/us/ttw

Contents

Introduction: Attention-Deficit/Hyperactivity Disorder (ADHD)
in Adolescence   *1*

Module 1   The Foundation: How to Better Organize and Plan

Chapter 1   Session 1: An Overview of This Treatment Program   *11*

Chapter 2   Session 2: How Can Parents Help? First
Parent/Adolescent Session   *29*

Chapter 3   Session 3: Do the Most Important Thing First!   *37*

Chapter 4   Session 4: What to Do When Things Aren't
Getting Done: Breaking Down Tasks and
Problem-Solving   *47*

Chapter 5   Session 5: How to Organize Everything   *53*

Module 2   How to Keep Going and Not Get Distracted

Chapter 6   Session 6: Figuring Out Your Attention Span and
Learning How to Delay Distractions   *61*

Chapter 7   Session 7: Optimize Your Setting   *69*

Module 3   How to Coach Yourself Better

Chapter 8   Session 8: Thinking, Feeling, and Acting   *79*

Chapter 9   Session 9: Self-Coaching   *93*

Chapter 10   Session 10: How Can Parents Help? Second
Parent/Adolescent Session   *103*

Chapter 11   Session 11: Don't Put It Off—Stop Procrastinating   *111*

Chapter 12   Session 12: Keeping It Going   *119*

Appendix   *125*

Bibliography   *151*

About the Authors   *153*

Introduction: Attention-Deficit/Hyperactivity Disorder (ADHD) in Adolescence

This introduction provides information about attention-deficit/hyperactivity disorder (ADHD) and how ADHD is diagnosed in adolescents, and it discusses the Cognitive Behavioral Model of ADHD. This information will help you decide if this treatment program is right for you.

- To understand the characteristics of ADHD in adolescence
- To learn why ADHD symptoms continue even after treatment with medications
- To understand that ADHD is a valid diagnosis for adolescents

What Is ADHD?

ADHD is a medical condition for which there are treatments and programs that can help. ADHD begins in childhood, though the symptoms affect you differently as a teenager. There are three major types of symptoms: inattention, hyperactivity, and impulsivity, as shown in Figure I.1.

The term "disinhibition" (lack of inhibition) is also sometimes used to describe the impulsivity and hyperactivity symptoms. Many adolescents with ADHD have at least some symptoms of poor attention, some symptoms of hyperactivity, and some symptoms of impulsivity, although many have symptoms that are primarily from one category.

1

SYMPTOMS OF INATTENTION

Being easily distracted
Having difficulty organizing
Becoming bored easily
Switching from one task to another
Having difficulty planning
Having difficulty concentrating
Having trouble doing boring
or unattractive tasks

SYMPTOMS OF HYPERACTIVITY

Feeling like one is driven by a motor
Feeling restless
Having difficulty sitting still
Always being "on the go"
Fidgeting

SYMPTOMS OF IMPULSIVITY

Interrupting often
Answering questions before the other
person finishes asking
Blurting out inappropriate comments
Acting before thinking
Doing things one later regrets
Having difficulty waiting

Figure I.1

Attention-deficit/hyperactivity disorder (ADHD) symptom domains.

The term "attention deficit disorder," or ADD is also sometimes used when someone has the attentional symptoms but not the hyperactivity symptoms.

ADHD Is Not Related to Intelligence or Laziness

ADHD is a problem that can lead to difficulties in your life. But you can learn coping skills to manage these difficulties. In 2006, Kate Kelly and Peggy Ramundo wrote a self-help book for adults with ADHD called *You Know I Am Not Lazy, Stupid, or Crazy?* The title of their book underscores many of the common misunderstandings that people with ADHD have about themselves.

We want to make sure that you understand that *ADHD is a neurobiological disorder*, unrelated to intelligence, laziness, aptitude, being or not being crazy, and so on. This treatment program, which typically begins after someone has been on ADHD medications, can help control the symptoms of ADHD. By actively learning skills and practicing them regularly, you will see significant improvements. From our perspective, the medicines can help "turn the volume down" on your symptoms, making it easier to learn the skills needed to manage your life.

What Are the Criteria for a Diagnosis of ADHD?

Generally, a diagnosis of ADHD is made by a mental health professional using the definition set forth by the American Psychiatric Association in its *Diagnostic and Statistical Manual of Mental Disorders*, 5th edition (DSM-5). The DSM-5 lists the symptoms and other requirements needed for individuals to qualify for all of the various psychiatric disorders.

In order to meet criteria for ADHD, individuals must have at least six symptoms out of the nine possible inattention symptoms and/or six symptoms out of the nine possible hyperactivity/impulsivity symptoms. If an individual has six or more symptoms in only the inattention category, we would say that person has ADHD, predominantly inattentive type. If they have six or more symptoms in the hyperactivity/impulsivity category, we would say that person has ADHD, predominantly hyperactive/impulsive type. If they have six or more symptoms in both categories, we would say that person has ADHD, combined type. In adults, only five of the nine symptoms are required in the inattentive, hyperactive/impulsive or combined presentations in order to meet full criteria for ADHD.

Inattentive symptoms include such things as not giving close attention to details, difficulty keeping your attention on tasks, seeming not to listen when someone is talking directly to you, having a hard time following through on instructions, having difficulties with organization, avoiding tasks that require continued mental effort, frequently losing things, getting distracted easily, and being forgetful.

Hyperactive/impulsive symptoms include fidgeting, leaving your seat frequently, feelings of restlessness, having a hard time with quiet activities, being always "on the go," talking excessively, blurting out answers, having difficulty waiting in lines, and frequently interrupting people.

In addition, a person needs to have had at least some of the symptoms before the age of 12, the symptoms need to be present in at least two different settings (for example, both at home and at school), the symptoms need to clearly interfere with the person's ability to function, and it must be clear that the symptoms are not better accounted for by something else.

How Do We Distinguish ADHD from Normal Functioning?

Some of the symptoms just listed sound like they might apply to almost anyone at certain times. For example, most people would probably say that they are sometimes easily distracted or sometimes have problems organizing. This is actually the case with many mental health problems. For example, everyone gets sad sometimes, but not everyone suffers from clinical depression. To diagnose anyone with ADHD, that person must have significant difficulties with some aspect of their life, such as work, school, or relationships.

Also, to qualify for a diagnosis of ADHD, the degree to which a person is upset or distressed, and the problems in their life that happen as a result of the symptoms must be caused by ADHD and not by another mental health problem. It is important to have a thorough assessment conducted to make sure that symptoms are not related to a different mental health or other medical health problem.

How Do Thoughts/Beliefs and Behaviors Make ADHD Worse for Adolescents?

Thoughts and beliefs can make ADHD symptoms worse. For example, a high schooler with ADHD who is facing something overwhelming might shift her attention elsewhere or think things like, "I can't do this," "I don't want to do this," or "I will do this later."

Behaviors are the things people do that can make ADHD symptoms worse. The actual behaviors can include things like avoiding doing what the person should be doing or not keeping an organizational system.

Later in this introduction, we show a model of how we believe ADHD affects people. According to this model, the core symptoms of ADHD are things that people are born with. However, we believe that cognitive and behavioral factors impact how much the symptoms get in the way of functioning.

- *Core neuropsychiatric impairments—starting in childhood—can prevent effective coping*: Adolescents with ADHD, by definition, have been suffering from this disorder chronically since childhood. Things such as distractibility, disorganization, difficulty following through on tasks, and impulsivity can prevent people with ADHD from learning or using effective coping skills.
- *Lack of effective coping can lead to underachievement and failures*: Because of these difficulties, many people with this disorder don't achieve as much as they could otherwise and therefore have experiences that they might label to themselves as "failures." We call these "perceived failures" because the person perceives it to be a failure, but maybe it actually isn't.
- *Underachievement and failures can lead to negative thoughts and beliefs*: This history of perceived failures can result in people with ADHD developing overly negative beliefs about themselves, as well as thinking that is too negative or not effective when approaching things that they need to do. The negative thoughts and beliefs that follow can lead to avoiding what they need to do, as well as getting distracted when they try to do things.
- *Negative thoughts and beliefs can lead to mood problems and can make avoidance more likely*: People with ADHD shift their attention even more when working on tasks or problems that they may find difficult or boring, and behaviors, such as avoidance, can get worse.
- *All of these factors added together lead to problems that affect your life*: When we say that people have "functional impairment," it means that they are not able to function as well as they should be able to. In adolescents, this can mean that people aren't doing as well as they could at school, they aren't getting along well with friends or family, or they aren't able to effectively participate in sports, play musical instruments, or pursue other hobbies. In short, they aren't able to do the things that they want, need to do, or might enjoy. This treatment is designed to address these issues and ultimately teach you skills so that you can function better.

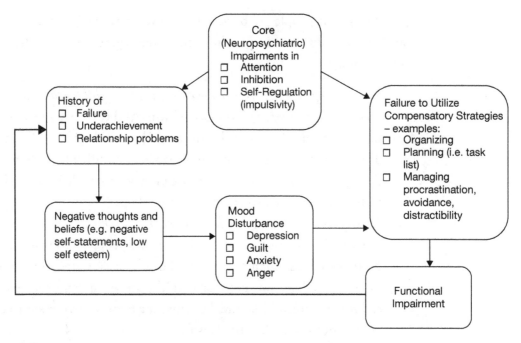

Figure I.2

Cognitive behavioral model of attention-deficit/hyperactivity disorder (ADHD).
Source: Originally published in Safren, S. A., Sprich, S., Chulvick, S., & Otto, M. W. (2004). Psychosocial treatments for adults with attention-deficit/hyperactivity disorder. *Psychiatric Clinics of North America, 27*(2), 349–360.

Figure I.2 is a model of how these factors relate to one another.

Don't Medications Effectively Treat ADHD?

Yes. Medications are currently the first-line treatment approach for ADHD, and they are the most extensively studied. The classes of these medications are stimulants, tricyclic antidepressants, monoamine oxidase inhibitors (antidepressants), and atypical antidepressants. However, for a lot of people, they don't do everything. A lot of people who are considered "responders" to these medicines show a reduction in only 50% or less of the core symptoms of ADHD. As noted earlier in this introduction, we consider medicines as a way to turn the volume down on your symptoms, making it easier for you to learn the organizing, planning, and the other skills in this workbook.

Recent data have emerged to suggest that combined medication and behavioral treatment has the best long-term results in terms of life problems in children with ADHD.

Because of these data, recommendations for the best treatment of adolescent ADHD include using psychotherapy (cognitive behavior therapy, in particular) in addition to medications. Medications can reduce many of the core symptoms of ADHD—attentional problems, high activity, and impulsivity—but the therapy can help people learn skills to reduce the impact that the symptoms have on their lives.

The approach that we present here in this workbook was tested on high school-aged students who were already diagnosed with ADHD and on medication for ADHD. We have found that it is important to inquire about regular medication use and to discuss the importance of taking medications as prescribed, so your therapist will be checking in with you about medication use throughout the treatment program. We have no reason to believe that this treatment would not be helpful for adolescents who are not taking medication for ADHD. However, as we keep saying, it is likely that medications turn the volume down on symptoms a bit, and make it easier to learn these CBT skills.

If Medications Work, Why Have This Cognitive Behavioral Treatment?

Medications alone cannot provide concrete strategies and skills for coping. Furthermore, disruptions in overall quality of life, such as problems at school and work and relationship difficulties associated with ADHD in adolescence, call for additional help to improve a person's quality of life.

Children with ADHD Do Grow Up

It is estimated that between 1% and 5% of adults have ADHD. This agrees with estimates that ADHD affects 2–9% of school-age children, and follow-up studies of children diagnosed with ADHD show that impairing ADHD symptoms last into adulthood (beyond adolescence) in 30–80% of diagnosed children.

Now that you have learned about adolescent ADHD and this program, you are ready to begin! You have already taken a big step by purchasing this workbook and making the decision to participate in this program. Let's get started!

The Foundation
How to Better Organize and Plan

CHAPTER 1

Session 1: An Overview of This Treatment Program

OVERVIEW

The first part of this chapter will provide you with information about how this program was developed to address specific concerns of adolescents with attention-deficit/hyperactivity disorder (ADHD) who are treated with medications. The chapter will also provide information about the success of the program in addressing these concerns and additional information about exactly what the program will involve.

GOALS

- Learn how this program was developed
- Learn about the concerns of medication-treated adolescents with ADHD
- Understand the success rate of the program so far
- Understand what the program will involve
- Understand the level of your ADHD symptoms as a basis for tracking treatment progress
- Discuss realistic goals
- Learn about this approach to treatment and the importance of practice, motivation, and staying with it
- Be introduced to using task lists and calendar systems
- Get started with task lists and calendar systems

This treatment program is meant to be completed with the assistance of a cognitive behavioral therapist. The treatment was developed by psychologists at the Massachusetts General Hospital's Cognitive Behavioral Therapy (CBT) Program (part of Harvard Medical School). It was based on the clinical experience of the authors, input from people living with ADHD, and from published works on treatment for adults and adolescents with ADHD. It is designed for individuals who have been diagnosed with ADHD, have been on medications for ADHD, and have found a stable medication plan. The strategies may be useful for adolescents with ADHD who cannot take medications, but we have only tested this program for individuals who were already taking medications.

How Was the Program Developed?

Clinical Experience of the Authors

The program was developed by a group of psychologists at Massachusetts General Hospital and Harvard Medical School after treating patients with ADHD in our clinic using CBT. From this perspective, it was originally developed based on the clinical experience of the authors, general principles of CBT, and published clinical guidelines for working with patients with ADHD.

Input from People Living with ADHD

Individuals with ADHD also gave input to the development of the treatment program. One of the authors interviewed a group of people with ADHD who had been taking medications about the types of problems they were experiencing and what they felt would be helpful skills for them to learn. The most frequently discussed problems among adult patients with ADHD who had been taking medicines were (1) organizing and planning, (2) distractibility, and (3) associated anxiety and depression. Other concerns included problems with procrastination, anger management, and communication issues. Examples will be discussed later.

Organizing and Planning

Problems with organizing and planning involve difficulties figuring out the logical, specific steps to complete tasks that seem overwhelming. For many people, this difficulty leads to giving up, procrastination, anxiety, and feelings of incompetence and underachievement. For example, several of our clients who were underemployed or unemployed had never completed thorough job searches, resulting in either not having a job or working in much lower paying positions than they could have.

For adolescents, difficulties in organizing and planning can lead to underachievement at school and missed deadlines (for example, missing the deadline to sign up for standardized tests or handing in assignments late). This treatment program is particularly helpful for these kinds of problems. Even though you have to invest time to set up the systems we suggest, once you start using them, it makes it so much easier to have free time that you can enjoy without worrying about your schoolwork.

Distractibility

Problems with distractibility involve problems at work or school. Many of our clients say that they do not complete tasks because other less important things get in the way.

Examples might include sitting down at one's computer to work on a project, but constantly going online to look up certain websites or visit social media sites. One of our clients, a student, always found himself cleaning his room every time he sat down to work on a difficult English paper or science project.

Distress (Associated Anxiety and Depression)

In addition to core ADHD symptoms, many of our clients have mood problems. These problems involve worry about events in their lives and sadness regarding either real underachievement or perceived underachievement. Many people with ADHD report a strong sense of frustration when they don't finish things or feel like they haven't done a good job on something.

Has This Treatment Program Been Successful?

Yes! In our first study of this treatment program in adults with ADHD, we found that people who completed this program in addition to taking their medications did significantly better than people who stayed on their medications but did not receive this treatment.

We conducted a *randomized controlled trial* to find these results. Randomized controlled trials are an important way that researchers test whether treatments work or not. They are *randomized* in that the people joining the study randomly receive either the actual treatment or a "comparison condition," such as a different treatment or perhaps no treatment.

In our first study, we only took in adults with ADHD who were being treated with medications and still had significant problems. These patients were randomized to either getting the treatment described in this book or no additional treatment (everyone continued on their prescribed medications). In this study, the people who got the treatment had significantly lower symptoms of ADHD after the treatment. This was evaluated by (1) what we call an *independent assessor*—someone who tested the participants but did not know whether the participants got the treatment or not—and (2) the participants themselves, who completed written questionnaires about their symptoms. According to these assessments, people who went through the program experienced about a 50% decrease in symptoms, and those who did not stayed pretty much the same.

Later, we conducted a larger 5-year study funded by a grant from the National Institute of Mental Health (to Dr. Safren), also using the first version of our treatment manual. This study involved comparing the treatment in the adult version of this manual (CBT) to a different treatment (*relaxation plus educational support* or RES). Eighty-six adults with ADHD who continued taking their medications participated in this study. We found that participants receiving CBT did better in terms of lowering their ADHD symptoms than did participants receiving RES, and there were more "responders" in the CBT group than the RES group, meaning that more people in the CBT group were considered significantly improved than in the RES group. These gains were maintained at 6- and 12-month follow-up.

While we were working on the trials with adults, we began adapting our program for use with adolescent clients. We felt that many of the skills that were helpful to our adult clients would be useful for our adolescent clients, but some changes needed to be made to reflect the different kinds of things that adolescents face. We therefore developed more specific content for adolescents and figured out what we thought would be the best way to involve parents (so that they could be most helpful).

To study how helpful this program would be with adolescents, we first tested it out with a few adolescents. We found that they generally liked it and that they experienced benefit from participation. This study laid the groundwork for our larger randomized study of this approach, which showed that CBT is an effective treatment for adolescents who have ADHD. Study participants included 46 teens between the ages of 14 and 18 with a primary diagnosis of ADHD who were on a steady dose of medication for ADHD. Participants completed 10 individual CBT sessions (with parents coming in for the last 10 minutes of each session) and 2 sessions which included both the adolescents and their parents for the full sessions. We also offered two optional sessions with parents only. We found that the adolescents showed improvements according to follow-up assessments by the teens themselves, by their parents, and by independent assessors.

What Will the Program Involve?

The Program Will Involve Regular Meetings with a Therapist and Home Practice of Skills

The treatment involves regular meetings with a cognitive behavioral therapist and home practice of the skills you work on. We have found that coming every week for these sessions works best. By having weekly sessions, you have a chance to practice the skills discussed in the treatment every week. Also, there is a relatively short period of time between sessions so that any problems with follow-through can be solved and any questions about the approach can be answered. When we have conducted sessions longer than a week apart, we find that clients report more difficulty because they would forget what they were supposed to be doing on their own.

The treatment is different from traditional psychotherapy. In fact, in some ways it is more like taking a course than being in therapy. Each session will have an agenda, and each session will have an associated activity for you to practice at home in between sessions. *Practice is essential.*

The Program Involves Practicing Outside of the Sessions!

There are no two ways about it! We have found that many clients have tried similar strategies in the past but have had difficulty integrating the skills into their daily lives. In other words, the tendency to be distractible and forgetful can get in the way of treatment. Your therapist will work with you to establish new habits. It probably will be annoying or hard at first—but we really do find that once you learn the skills (1) they get easier and become a habit and (2) they make it so you are more effective when you have to work so that (3) you are able to have and enjoy more free time to do what you want! You will need to practice these new skills long enough for them to become habits. Once they have become habitual, they will be easy to use and remember.

You may be tempted to quit, but maybe not as much at the beginning when you are first starting. People typically do not quit at the beginning. The middle period can sometimes be the hardest. This is when the novelty wears off, but people have not practiced the skills long enough for them to become habits. Many people show some improvement at the beginning, enough so they start to think that they do not need to use the skills. In this case, people may quit (because it is no longer new and interesting and because the skills have not yet become habits), but then they relapse back to having problems. They then think, "I tried to change and I could not do it." In this way, the cycle of negative emotions and continued ADHD symptoms persists. Do not give in to the temptation to quit!

This may be the hardest part of the treatment program. The key to getting better is to stay on track and stick with the program long enough for the skills to really help you.

You Will Have Ups and Downs and Sometimes Setbacks When Doing This Program

When there is a "down," this is definitely not the time to quit. Rather, this is the time to learn from the things that led up to the setback and figure out how to handle them in the future. This is extremely important. Try to remind yourself that setbacks are a major part of progress. You need to have setbacks and learn to handle them to reduce the likelihood that you will have setbacks in the future!

The final period of treatment might be easier. However, it can also involve challenges. Once things are going better, you will be faced with the challenge of continuing to invest some time and energy into maintaining these systems and skills *even though things will be going better*!

We have found that some people, once they are doing better, feel less motivated to keep using the coping skills. If things are bad, then there is more motivation because people feel the need to "get out of the hole." But when things are going well, some people lose their motivation, which can lead to setbacks.

The treatment involves four core modules: (1) information/organizing and planning, (2) coping with distractibility, (3) adaptive thinking, and (4) parent/adolescent sessions. In addition, we include an optional session on procrastination and two optional parent-only sessions, plus a session on how to maintain gains following the end of treatment.

The Foundation—How to Better Organize and Plan

The first part of the treatment involves organization and planning skills. This includes skills such as:

- Learning to effectively and consistently use a calendar
- Learning to effectively and consistently use a task list
- Working on effective problem-solving skills, including (1) breaking down tasks into steps and (2) choosing a best solution for a problem when no solution is ideal
- Developing a good system for sorting and keeping necessary papers or emails
- Developing organizational systems for papers, electronic files, and other items

How to Keep Going and Not Get Distracted

The second part of treatment involves managing distractibility. Skills include the following:

- Determining a reasonable length of time that you can expect to focus on boring or difficult tasks and breaking tasks down into chunks that match this length of time
- Using a timer, cues, and other techniques that you will learn

How to Coach Yourself Better

The third part of treatment involves learning to think about problems and stressors in the most helpful/effective way possible. This includes:

- Positive "self-coaching"
- Learning how to identify and dispute negative, overly positive, and/or unhelpful thoughts
- Learning how to look at situations rationally and therefore make rational choices about the best possible solutions

Parent/Adolescent Sessions

The sessions with the parent(s) and adolescent are designed to provide information to your parent(s) about ADHD and the treatment program, to make sure that you and your parent(s) are "on the same page" in terms of your goals for treatment and, depending on your age, to develop a reward system to help you to stay motivated. These sessions can also be used to discuss school accommodations if needed. The parents are also brought in at the end of all individual sessions for a few minutes just so that they can be aware of the skills that you are working on and can help you outside of the treatment sessions.

Don't Put It Off—Stop Procrastinating

Chapter 11 is an optional session covering procrastination. We include this even though most of the previous sessions relate to procrastination, but some people require extra help in this area. This session therefore specifically points to how to use the preceding skills to help with procrastination.

Parent-Only Sessions

The optional parent-only sessions can be scheduled at your parents' request if they feel that it would be helpful for them to get some coaching from your therapist or if they have things that they would like to discuss with your therapist. You and your therapist might decide that it would be helpful for your therapist to talk with your parents without you present, and he could suggest that one or more parent-only sessions be scheduled.

The Program Will Involve Monitoring Your Progress

Before starting this program, your therapist will likely have done a diagnostic interview to establish whether or not you have ADHD. Part of the treatment approach described in this workbook involves regularly monitoring your improvement. Because, unlike many medical illnesses, we do not have a blood test for symptom severity, we need to use the next best thing, which is a self-report symptom checklist of your ADHD symptoms. Your therapist will have you complete this. You should complete this checklist around the time of your first session and then complete it again each week at the start of your therapy session so that you can monitor your progress and so that you can focus on areas that may not be improving at the level you would like. Your therapist may also give you a questionnaire to measure *functional impairment*, which has less to do with symptoms and more to do with how you are functioning in various areas of your life like schoolwork, family relationships, social relationships, and hobbies.

The Program Will Involve Setting an Agenda for Each Treatment Session

To ensure that important material is covered, you and your therapist will set an agenda for each and every therapy session. This way you can cover all the material that is presented in this book.

Potential Pitfalls with Modular Treatment

Remember: not everything can be covered at once. Although the treatment approach is offered one module at a time, you may have areas of difficulty that will not be addressed until future sessions.

This is another issue that is sometimes frustrating for people who do this program. The program typically starts with the development of a calendar and task list system. That module also involves learning organization and planning skills. The next module looks at distractibility. People sometimes have problems with the first module because they get easily distracted, but distractibility is not covered until the next module. Unfortunately, it is impossible to learn everything all at once, so we ask that you do your best, but we realize that you will not have learned all the necessary skills until the end of the treatment program.

The Program Will Involve Repetition

There are many areas of the treatment where we repeat key information. We do this because repetition is the best way to learn new information. Each module contains new information and also contains information from previous modules that it is important to review.

The Program Will Involve Using Specific Strategies for Remembering to Take Medication (If You Are Currently Taking Medication)

For some people with ADHD, taking medication every day, sometimes more than once a day, can be difficult. Symptoms of ADHD such as distractibility or poor organization may interfere, causing you to forget to take all of your prescribed doses or to have difficulty developing a structured routine for taking medication. This treatment will help you with this and will provide you with opportunities to work with a therapist and problem-solve around difficulties taking medications. If you have difficulties, you will have the opportunity to discuss factors leading to missed doses and try to come up with a plan to avoid this in the future.

Orientation to the Foundation: How to Better Organize and Plan so You Can Have and Enjoy Your Free Time

The second part of this chapter will help you come up with goals for therapy that are both specific and within your control. In addition, you will learn the skills that will allow you to get started with your own personalized task list and calendar systems.

Symptom Checklist

ADHD symptom checklists include each of the symptoms of ADHD so you can rate yourself. Each week of treatment will involve working on specific ADHD symptoms. As you go through the treatment, you should expect to see a gradual decrease in your symptoms. If there are specific sets of symptoms that do not seem to be changing, you should focus on these areas.

Tracking your symptoms on a weekly basis can also help you become more aware of these difficulties. Being aware that these are symptoms of ADHD, doing this self-assessment regularly, and tracking the changes can also be helpful on its own. This awareness can help you remember to use the skills that you will be learning in future sessions.

Your therapist will give you an ADHD symptom checklist to complete now. Pay particular attention to the items that have the highest ratings as these are important for treatment. Then fill in your score and today's date on the lines just below:

Score: _____   **Date:** _____

Medication Adherence

Using the ADHD Medication Form, record your prescribed dosage of medication and indicate the number of doses you actually took. Think about reasons for any missed doses, such as being distracted, running out of medication, your parents forgetting to give you your medication, or your thoughts about not wanting/needing to take medication. You should repeat this exercise at the beginning of every therapy session and share it with your therapist so that it can be discussed in therapy.

ADHD Medication Form

How many times were you supposed to take your ADHD medicine this week? _____

How many times did you actually take your ADHD medicine this week? _____

Reasons for missed doses: _____

_____

_____

Goals for Cognitive Behavioral Therapy for ADHD

You have just completed a checklist of the symptoms that are typical of ADHD in adolescents. We find that reviewing this list can also help you think about individual goals that you might have related to which types of problems most affect you. Additionally, it might help you think about how they actually interfere in your life.

Part of getting started on this course of CBT for ADHD is making sure you have realistic goals for the treatment. Realistic goals for CBT for ADHD are things that you can control.

Being Realistic and "Controllability"

You might be thinking that a long-term (or medium-term) goal of yours is to get into college (or a good college). This is a great goal, and we believe the skills described in this workbook can help you increase the chances of meeting it. However, the outcome of getting into college depends on lots of other factors that you do not directly control (such as how many people apply to each college and how many other students from your school apply to the same college). A more realistic goal would therefore be to figure out what steps are necessary to improve the chances of you getting into a college that is good for you and acting on these steps.

There are likely areas related to ADHD that are also preventing you from doing the things that would help you get into a college that would be a good fit for you. These areas might include figuring out effective ways to study, improving your organizational skills so that you don't forget to do homework assignments, and prioritizing your work so that the most important assignments always get completed. These are issues that the treatment can help with because you can directly control them.

Questions to Help Come Up with Goals

The following questions may be helpful with respect to coming up with goals regarding your treatment:

- What made you decide to start this treatment now? (You can say "Because my parents made me," but are there other reasons—for you—that you went along with it?)
- What types of things would you like to be different regarding how you approach tasks?
- What are some issues that other people have noticed about how you approach things?
- If you did not have problems with ADHD anymore, what do you think would be different in your life?

Write down *your* goals for CBT using Worksheet 1: Goals of CBT, which is located in the Appendix at the end of this workbook. There are also columns for controllability and whether the goal is short- or long-term.

Goal of CBT	Controllability (as a percent)	Short or long term
Get into a good college	65%	Long
Learn how to stop procrastinating	90%	Short
Be more organized with my homework and my stuff	95%	Short
Get along better with my parents	50%	Short and Long

Figure 1.1

Example goals of cognitive behavioral therapy (CBT)

For controllability, write down how much control you think you have over this goal, even if the ADHD symptoms were gone (0% represents no control; 100% represents complete control). This part you can discuss with your therapist. Also indicate whether this is a short-term or long-term goal.

We ask you to rate controllability (and as already noted, this should be done with a therapist) so that you can gain a realistic idea of your goals for CBT. For example, a goal might be to make the varsity soccer team, but there are many factors that impact this goal that are not within your control, like how many other kids try out for the team and how skillful they are at soccer. Therefore, we prefer to have a related goal that is more controllable, such as jog three times per week and lift weights twice per week.

Review the goals and the controllability ratings. Ask yourself if there are specific areas that you can control about each situation and if there are specific areas that are beyond your control. Figure 1.1 shows an example goal list.

Additional Information About This Approach to Treatment

As we have discussed, this treatment is made up of different modules or sections that each target different sets of skills. In other words, it is designed so that each skill builds on previously learned skills. You will be learning one technique at a time. As you begin this treatment program, there are several things to keep in mind about how the treatment is structured.

- *The therapy is active*: First, due to difficulties known to be associated with ADHD, the therapy will be especially active; almost like taking a class. Each session will have an agenda which you and your therapist will discuss at the beginning of the session.

- *The therapy requires practice outside of sessions*: Each session will involve a review of the things you have already learned and are working on, as well as discussing new coping strategies and trying them out for the next week. The more you are able to do this, the better the results you will see.

- *The therapy works on one skill at a time*: This means that you will have areas of difficulty that are not addressed right away. For example, the first module (Chapters 1–5) is on organizing and planning. The second (Chapters 6–7) is on distractibility. Of course, organizing and planning things are much easier if you do not become distracted. Likewise, if we started with distractibility, it would be difficult to figure out what you were getting distracted from if you were not organized. Therefore, it is important to realize that only one thing at a time can be changed, and the key is to practice things long enough so that you can really tell if they will be helpful to you.

- *Practice makes perfect*: You are about to start a treatment for problems that involve difficulties with follow-through. Some or all of these skills may seem difficult. This is why you will be doing the treatment with a therapist and not on your own, and this is also why it is critical to know right from the start how important it is to practice these new skills. Remember Figure I.2, the Cognitive Behavioral Model of ADHD, which appears in the Introduction to this workbook. Many people with ADHD never get a chance to learn coping skills because they quit practicing a skill before they have practiced it enough for it to become a habit!

- *Motivation is key*: Your therapist will be working with you to help you understand exactly how each skill may be useful for you. Your therapist will also be working to make sure that you are working on goals that are important for you. Be sure to let your therapist know if there are times when you are confused about how a particular skill might be useful for you, or if you are feeling that your therapist does not understand your goals. By doing this, you can get the most out of the treatment program.

If you participate in this program, there will certainly be some challenges. At times, it will likely be difficult to maintain your motivation to change your behaviors. Try to remember that this program is for your own benefit and that you are doing it in order to decrease the strain that your ADHD symptoms put on your everyday life. That being said, in order to get the most out of the treatment, you should think about the fact that the treatment is giving you tools to increase the quality of your life rather than looking at the treatment as a set of extra tasks that your therapist is asking you to do. You really need to put in the time and effort yourself because no one else can change your habits for you.

Skill: Using a Calendar and Task List

Calendar and task list systems are very important for organization. These are absolutely necessary. Although there are other things you also need in order to be organized, these things are critical. We consider this to be similar to needing to eat to stay healthy. There are also many other things that you need to do to stay healthy, such as going to the doctor, taking medicine if you get an infection, and so on. Eating is a necessary—but not sufficient—requirement for health. We believe that maintaining a calendar and task list system are necessary—but not sufficient—requirements for being organized.

Using the Calendar and Task List Together

Even though we give specific recommendations, the calendar system and task list systems can be personalized. Many people say that they have tried to use a calendar system in the past but it has not worked, or they did not keep up with it. Remember, the goal of this treatment is to try things long enough for them to become automatic habits. Every week from here on out, you will be asked to use skills that build on the use of the calendar and task list system. These two systems can be used together. Also, they can be electronic—on your phone, tablet, or computer—or on paper. If you use systems on your phone, it is typically helpful to have systems that are linked to your computer and stored on the cloud. This way, if you lose your phone, leave it behind, misplace it, or it breaks, you can always access the calendar/task list or have a backup.

- *The task list* will contain information about things or tasks that you need to do but that are not tied to a specific date. The task list should replace having random pieces of paper or electronic notes that can be easily lost.

- *The calendar* is your key to remembering when you have to do things, like keeping appointments and/or the dates for things like tests, quizzes, or long-term assignments for school. When using the calendar with the task list, you may place items from the task list onto specific days or times on the calendar.

Rules for the Calendar and Task List

1. *The calendar and task list replace* all *pieces of paper and random electronic notes.*
   - Pieces of paper just get lost, and electronic notes can be misplaced easily.
   - Instead of keeping an appointment slip, a business card, or anything like this, copy the information onto the task list or enter it directly into your calendar.

2. *All appointments, teacher meetings, sports practices, school concerts, etc. go on the calendar.*
   - No papers, flyers, or appointment cards that can easily get lost!

3. *Homework and other tasks must go onto the task list.*
   - The task list is something that will be further developed in future chapters. This is a key component of the program.
   - Look at the task list *every day* and revise it accordingly.
   - If you have a separate electronic or study-skills system for your homework, use this task list in conjunction with that.

4. *Do not obsess about trying to get a perfect system.*
   - Many individuals want to have perfect systems. Do not fall into this trap, which will just result in not having any systems at all!
   - If you cannot decide on the "best" system, then just use a simple calendar and task list system.
   - Remember, it's important to give your system a fair shot! This means keeping one system for at least 3 months, long enough to get used to it.

5. *Use a system that is within your comfort zone.*
   - There are many, many options for different calendar and task list systems—including paper systems, apps on smartphones or tablets, and multiple computerized applications. Many of our clients ask us which is the "best" system, and this is not

really a question that we can easily answer. The question for you to ask yourself is really "What is the best system for me?"

You need to consider whether you are allowed to have your phone or tablet out at school when you need to enter in assignments. Also, you should think about the ease of using an electronic system versus the fact that electronic devices have a greater potential to provide distractions than do paper systems. It is important that you always have your systems with you to enter appointments or tasks so that you don't forget them.

Potential Pitfalls

It is important to remember that learning any new skill takes practice and takes time. You may not be used to writing down appointments or carrying around your task list and calendar systems. Be aware of thoughts that may sabotage your success down the road, such as:

"I don't have room in my bag for my tablet or smartphone."

"I've never been an organized person, why start now?"

"If I write down my appointments and assignments, I will need to do them."

You will be learning ways to manage these thinking traps in later chapters. For now, try to keep focused on your reasons for beginning this program, the goals you hope to achieve, and the sense of accomplishment you will feel for taking positive steps in your life.

Practice

- Create an organizational system with a calendar and a task list following the rules listed earlier.
- Put all appointments in the calendar and start *one* master task list.
- Read over the materials for the next session.

CHAPTER 2

Session 2: How Can Parents Help? First Parent/Adolescent Session

OVERVIEW

This single chapter will help you work with your parent(s) to better manage your attention-deficit/hyperactivity disorder (ADHD) symptoms. As we discussed in Chapter 1, this treatment program is best done with the help of a therapist who is familiar with cognitive behavioral therapy (CBT). We therefore recommend that you and your parent(s) meet together with the therapist for one session to go over the material presented in the Introduction and Chapter 1 and to discuss any other background information that might be useful.

This combined parent–adolescent session can take place at any time between Sessions 2 and 6. The primary goals are to provide information about the treatment to your parent(s) and to make sure that everyone is "on the same page" about the treatment. You can talk with your therapist about what makes the most sense in terms of the treatment, and you can talk with your parent(s) about their schedule and then plan accordingly.

Involving parents in the treatment will enable you to

- Gain support as you complete treatment, and
- Decrease any tension in your relationship related to ADHD symptoms.

- Provide education about ADHD
- Provide an overview of the CBT model of the continuation of ADHD into adulthood
- Get feedback from parents on symptom severity
- Discuss organization and planning techniques
- Discuss coping with distractibility techniques
- Discuss adaptive (effective) thinking techniques
- Discuss the role of parents in the treatment
- Talk about parent goals for the treatment and set realistic expectations
- Develop a motivational/reward system (if applicable)
- Agree on home practice activities

Education About ADHD and Overview of CBT Model

The goal of this portion of the session is for your therapist to provide your parents with the educational information that was presented to you in the first treatment session. Your therapist will review the information about the myths about ADHD and introduce the Cognitive Behavioral Model of ADHD. Your therapist will discuss some of the techniques that will be used during treatment, such as the task list and calendar systems. Your therapist will also talk about the need to practice skills at home and how this relates to the success of the program.

Symptom Checklist with Parent Feedback

ADHD symptom checklists contain each of the symptoms of ADHD so you can rate yourself. Each week of treatment will involve working on specific ADHD symptoms. As you go through the treatment, you should expect to see a gradual decrease in symptom severity. If there are specific sets of symptoms that do not seem to be changing, you should focus on these areas.

Tracking your symptoms on a weekly basis can also help you become more aware of these difficulties. Being aware that these are symptoms of ADHD, doing this self-assessment regularly, and tracking the changes can also be helpful on its own. This awareness can help you remember to use the skills that you will be learning in future sessions.

Your therapist will give you an ADHD symptom checklist to complete now. Pay particular attention to the items that have the highest ratings as these are important for treatment. Then fill in your score and today's date on the lines below.

Score: _____   **Date:** _____

We usually ask the parent(s) to complete a Symptom Checklist as another way to report on progress. If you are willing, we would like to have your parent(s) complete one, and we can compare ratings to see if they are similar.

Medication Adherence

Using the ADHD Medication Form, record your prescribed dosage of medication and indicate the number of doses you actually took. Think about reasons for missed doses such as being distracted, running out of medication, your parents forgetting to give you your medication, or your thoughts about not wanting/needing to take medication. You should repeat this exercise at the beginning of every therapy session and share it with your therapist so that it can be discussed in therapy.

ADHD Medication Form

How many times were you supposed to take your ADHD medicine this week? _____

How many times did you actually take your ADHD medicine this week? _____

Reasons for missed doses: _____

_____

_____

In this session, your therapist can get input from your parent(s) about any thoughts that they might have about things that get in the way of you taking your medications and also problem-solve around how your parents might be helpful in reminding you to take your medications, if needed.

Overview of Treatment for Parents

Your therapist will quickly preview the skills that will be taught in this treatment program and discuss with your parents how the skills can relate to the effect of ADHD on family relationships. While discussing the modules, the therapist may ask your parents how they think they could help you to use the various skills.

1. The Foundation—How to Better Organize and Plan

The central goal of this first set of sessions (Chapters 1–5) is to develop a complete system for organizing and planning. This means consistently using a calendar and task list system (looking at the task list and calendar daily), learning problem-solving skills, and managing organization. Areas in which the parents can help may include:

- Assuring that important family events get put into the calendar
- Assisting with prioritization of tasks, and, if a mutually agreed on important task arises, making sure that it gets put onto the task list
- Helping to find a place for important items (backpack, laptop, homework, cell phone), and, if these items are seen elsewhere, moving them back to the designated place or alerting you to the fact that they are out of place
- Helping to purchase items for organizational systems
- Providing positive feedback

2. How to Keep Going and Not Get Distracted

The central goal of this set of sessions (Chapters 6–7) is to learn tools for coping with distractibility. This involves learning about the length of one's attention span and breaking down tasks into steps that take that amount of time. It also involves learning skills like "distractibility delay" and modifying one's environment so that work can be done efficiently.

3. How to Coach Yourself Better

The central goal of this set of sessions (Chapters 8–10) is to learn to think more adaptively or effectively about situations or tasks. This involves learning to identify one's thoughts, look at the relationship between thoughts and mood, identify evidence for or against the thought, and then develop an alternate way of thinking about the situation or task.

Parent(s) Role in Treatment

At this point, your therapist will try to engage you and your parents in a discussion about the role that your parents will play in this treatment program. The role that they play will depend on many factors, including your age and your current level of independence. For example, if you are in middle school, you probably rely on your parents to make appointments for you, drive you around to activities, and so on. Your parents may also communicate directly with your school. On the other hand, if you are a senior in high school or already in college, you may be more independent in making your own appointments, getting to activities on your own, and so on. Parent involvement will also depend on how well you have been able to communicate in the past and how frustrated each family member is currently feeling. You should share your thoughts and wishes about this at this meeting. Sometimes it is easier to talk about these issues with a therapist present and to come up with a "game plan" that you can try. There will be opportunities to change the game plan in the future if it isn't working well, so don't feel that the plan you come up with during this session will be the plan that you need to stick to forever.

Discussion of Parent Goals for Treatment and Setting Realistic Expectations

Your therapist will talk with your parents about their goals for this treatment program. Your therapist will work with your parents to make sure that their goals are realistic. For example, if they are hoping that you will get better grades but you are already halfway through the school year, it may be difficult to pull your grades up significantly by the end of the year. It is important for everyone to realize that this does not mean you are not making progress; rather, it means that it takes time to make major changes.

You can share your own goals for the program with your parents at this time. You and your parents can compare the goals that you set with the goals that they set and talk about ways in which the goals are similar or different. The hope is that you and your parents will leave the session being on the same page about why you are doing this treatment. You will revisit these goals at the second parent/adolescent session later in the treatment.

Development of Motivational Reward System (If Applicable)

At this session, you and your parents should discuss whether you want to try to have some type of reward system to help you keep up your motivation to learn and use the new skills from the program. The goal of this system is not for your parents to "bribe" you, but rather to help you stay motivated and to recognize that it is very difficult to change your behavior and it requires a lot of hard work. Not everyone wants to have a reward system, so it is not required—just something that we put forth for you to consider.

If you decide that a reward system would be helpful, you should collaborate with your parents to figure out what behaviors will be rewarded. The more specific you can be, the better. For example, it's not that helpful if you agree that "good grades" will be rewarded. Something more specific, like "writing down your homework assignments in your planner every day," is much better since that is something you can easily determine. The goal is that the system will help you establish better patterns or habits, which will then become more automatic as time goes on.

In terms of rewards, you should look at things that you don't normally get to have or do. If you normally have access to video games whenever you want, being allowed to play a video game wouldn't really feel like a reward. Depending on your age, a reward could be anything from going out to dinner or for ice cream, going to a movie or an amusement park with a friend, extra privileges, or gift cards from a store. You should make the system fairly simple. Figure out a check-in time each day when you can agree on whether or not you did what you had agreed upon, and then another check-in each week when you decide on your reward for that week. If the system is too complicated, it is more likely that you and your parents will stop using it regularly.

As you are learning in this treatment, practicing new skills is vital so that you become familiar with them, are able to easily use the tools, and begin to see the positive results that can emerge when you consistently use these CBT strategies. Recognize that, at first, when you are learning a new skill, it may feel awkward, may be confusing, and may require effort to implement. That's ok! The more you practice, the easier it will become.

- With your parents, continue to discuss ways in which your parent(s) can provide support while you are in treatment.
- Read over the materials for the next session.

CHAPTER 3

Session 3: Do the Most Important Thing First!

OVERVIEW

The main focus of this chapter is to teach you how to manage multiple tasks. It is important for you to remember that practice makes perfect. Although these techniques may seem unfamiliar at first, over time they will become more automatic. Even if you feel frustrated, it is important for you to stick with the techniques until they become habits.

GOALS

- Continue to monitor your progress
- Review your use of the calendar and task list
- Learn how to manage multiple tasks
- Learn how to prioritize tasks
- Problem-solve regarding any potential difficulties using this technique
- Agree on home practice activities and anticipate difficulties using these techniques

Review of Symptom Checklist

As you have been doing each week, you should complete the attention-deficit/hyperactivity disorder (ADHD) symptom checklist that you and your therapist are using to track your symptoms. Be sure to review your score and take note of symptoms that have improved and those that are still problematic and share this information with your therapist.

Score: _____ Date: _____

Review of Medication Adherence

Using the ADHD Medication Form, record your prescribed dosage of medication and indicate the number of doses you actually took. Think about reasons for missed doses, such as being distracted, running out of medication, your parents forgetting to give you your medication, or your thoughts about not wanting/needing to take medication. You should repeat this exercise at the beginning of every therapy session and share it with your therapist so that it can be discussed in therapy.

ADHD Medication Form

How many times were you supposed to take your ADHD medicine this week? _____

How many times did you actually take your ADHD medicine this week? _____

Reasons for missed doses: _____

_____

_____

Review of Previous Chapters

Each week you should examine your progress in using the skills that you have learned so far in this treatment. It is important to acknowledge the successes you have achieved and to problem-solve around any difficulties.

Review: Tools for Organization and Planning

- Use of calendar for managing appointments
- Use of task list system

Remember, having a good calendar and task list system is *necessary* (but not sufficient) to get organized.

If you have not yet decided on systems to use to keep track of appointments, meetings, practices, and tasks, this should be your top priority. Try to figure out how to problem-solve getting started with your systems by experimenting with different calendars and task lists to decide which one works best for you. Remember, in order for this treatment to be successful, it is important that you have the proper tools!

If you have started to use new calendar and task list systems, review these specifics:

- How will you remember to look at your calendar every day?
- When will you add important schoolwork/long-term assignments into the calendar (like tests, quizzes, papers, or projects due)? Will you add them as they are assigned, or one time per week?
- How will you remember to look at your task list every day? We find that picking a certain time every day is the best—for example, when you feed your dog, after you brush your teeth, when you go online for the first time in the morning, when you first arrive at school, or while you are having breakfast. As you are forming this new habit, it may help to have the list in plain view or to set a reminder to look at the list around the time that you need to look at it each day.
- Think about how you want to integrate these systems. For example, you may want to have tasks on your task list and also designate specific "appointment times" on your calendar when you are scheduling yourself to complete the tasks.

Remember, just because you have a task list, it doesn't mean that you have to complete all of the items on the list immediately! It is simply a tool that is going to help you become organized and avoid forgetting things that are not on the list. The calendar and task lists are the building blocks for the rest of the treatment program. It is essential that you make a plan to look at them *every day*!

When looking at the task list and the calendar, you may notice that you often need to manage multiple tasks at one time. This is especially true for students who have assignments for many different classes (both short-term homework and long-term papers or projects) as well as personal tasks (buying birthday gifts for friends, looking for a part-time job) and future-oriented tasks (studying for the SAT and/or the ACT, completing college applications, taking Driver's Education classes).

When you have ADHD, it can become difficult to figure out what you should do first. Even if you have decided that a particular task is important, it is often difficult to stick with it until it is completed.

In the following exercise, you will learn a concrete strategy to help you decide which tasks are most important. This technique is one example of how you can "force yourself" to organize tasks.

Master List Versus Daily List

It is important to have both a "master list" that holds all of the tasks that need to be completed in general, as well as a "daily list" of tasks that you are actually hoping to complete on a particular day. You can divide the list up into different sections, such as school and home, if desired.

All tasks should remain on the master list until they have been completed. If a task on the daily list does not get completed that day, it should be moved to the next day's list. Many electronic systems allow items to be assigned a particular date, and the item will automatically move to the following day if it has not been checked off as having been completed. This can also be done using a paper system. It is really important that you find a system that works for you and that also works with your school. If your school has a website or learning platform, you can work with that system. If you prefer to use a paper planner, use that. The most important thing is that you start using one system consistently.

Skill: Prioritizing

When you are faced with a number of tasks that you must do, it is important to have a clear strategy for prioritizing which tasks are most important so that you make sure that the most important tasks are sure to get completed.

The best way that we know of to do this is to *rate* each task. We find that people like to complete easier tasks first. This can be problematic because the easier tasks are often the tasks that are not as important. When we do this, we feel that we are getting things accomplished, but we also find that we are never making progress on our important goals. For example, Peter (a student who we know) is really good at math, but he has a hard time with reading—especially for homework. Math homework, for Peter, is easy because he can just do one problem at a time and plow through. History and science are harder because he has to read the material, understand it, and then go back and figure out answers to the questions on the reading. Or, worse for Peter, he has to write short essays in response. Because he dreads this, he does the math first. However, when it comes time to do the history or science, he is a bit more tired because he just spent so much time on the math, and he wants to stop doing homework for the day. For Peter, it is better to do the harder stuff first, when he has more energy and is ready to begin, and then do the math last, when his energy level has decreased a little and when it is later in the evening and his medications have worn off a bit.

When prioritizing tasks, it is important that you not rely solely on due dates and timelines to determine importance. You should also think about how long you expect the task to take you to complete and if it is likely to cause you stress. For example, if writing is difficult for you and takes you longer than other types of assignments, prioritize getting started on an essay or term paper over easy homework assignments that are due sooner. This will remind you to start the writing assignment earlier than you think you need to and relieve some of the stress that you are likely to experience around getting this assignment done.

Skill: The "A, B, Cs"

List all of your tasks. Then assign an "A," "B," or "C" rating to each task.

- *"A" Tasks*: These are the tasks of highest importance. This means that they must be completed in the short term (like today or tomorrow).

    For example: "Complete science worksheet that is due tomorrow."

- *"B" Tasks*: These are lower importance, longer term tasks, some portions of which should be completed in the short term, but the other portions may take longer.

    For example: "Write outline for English essay that is due in 2 weeks."

- *"C" Tasks*: These are the lowest importance tasks; they may be more attractive and easier to do, but they are not as important.

    For example: "Decorate sign to take to basketball game on Friday night."

Work with your therapist to generate a task list and discuss ratings for each item. Be very careful not to rate too many items as "A."

The "A," "B," "C" strategy can be applied both to the master list and to the daily list. In the case of the master list, you can use it to decide which items are most important and need to go on that day's list. In the case of the daily list, use it to decide which item to do first, which to do second, and so on.

You will see that the priority ratings sometimes change over time. For example, an essay that needs to be completed in the distant future may be placed on your master list, and you might rate it as a "C." However, as the deadline approaches, you may choose to work on a small section of the essay on a particular day and change the rating to a "B," and then finally set out to finish the essay and change the rating to an "A" if you have not yet completed it. Sometimes, events will occur that may cause you to modify your ratings (for example, your teacher asking you to hand in a rough draft of your essay 2 weeks ahead of the final deadline).

Skill: Using This Technique

You can now add the "A," "B," "C" technique to the tool box of skills that you are developing to combat your ADHD symptoms. In addition to making a "to do" list for each day, you should now assign a rating of "A," "B," or "C" to each task. You should do *all* of the "A" tasks before doing *any* of the "B" tasks!! This may be hard for you, but it is very important! It will help you make sure that you complete the tasks that are important to you. Remember that sometimes the higher priority tasks represent only a step toward a larger goal. Using Peter's example from our earlier discussion, note that he doesn't need to write the entire essay before moving on to the next task; he only needs to write the outline (the portion that was set as the goal for that day) before moving on to the next task.

If this strategy doesn't work for you, try simply assigning numbers to each of your daily tasks, from most important to least important, and then completing them in that order. This helps you make sure that you are getting the most important tasks done even if you run out of time and aren't able to finish everything on your list.

Use this technique every day. Get in the habit of pausing to assess what you need to do and to carefully decide what you should start with, what you should do second, and so on. By practicing this technique regularly, you will ensure that the most important tasks get completed and that you don't end your days with regrets.

Skill: Use of Rewards to Increase Motivation

Think about what motivates you and how you can use this information to help you complete tasks. For example, there is something called the *Premack Principle*, which says that a low-frequency behavior (something you don't do often—and perhaps don't enjoy doing) will increase in frequency if it is made contingent on a high-frequency behavior (that is, if you tie it in with something you do often and enjoy). Think about how you usually end up spending your time and/or what you like to spend time doing and use this information to help you complete tasks (such as homework or chores) that are less interesting or fun. For example, you might try setting up an "if . . . then" rule such as, "*If* I finish this history reading assignment—pages 55–67—*then* I can watch some videos or an episode of a show." Be specific about both the task that needs to be completed and the rewarding activity.

You can also think about whether it would be useful if you could work out a "reward system" with your parents. This would be something that you and your parents would agree upon, with the goal of helping you increase your motivation to do something that is difficult for you. You and your therapist can discuss this with your parents at the end of the session if you like.

Potential Pitfalls

You may be feeling that we are asking you to do a lot, but don't get discouraged! You are trying to learn new skills, and it will take some time before the skills become habits. As you become accustomed to using your task list, you will learn more about how much is realistic for you to expect to do in one day.

At this point, if you find that you are not finishing all of the items on your list, simply move the things that haven't been completed to the next day's list and re-rate them the next day. Don't forget: leave all tasks on the "master list" until they have been completed. In later chapters, you may want to problem-solve if you are finding that you are consistently not finishing the most important items on your list.

Remember, at this point, you are just trying to get in the habit of using the task list every day and making sure that you are doing the most important tasks first.

Practice

As you are learning in this treatment, practicing new skills is vital so that you become familiar with them, are able to easily use the tools, and begin to see the positive results that can emerge when you consistently use these CBT strategies. Recognize that, at first, when you are learning a new skill, it may

	Task	Date Put on List	Date Completed
A	Review homework planner		
A	Write outline for English paper		
.	Do math homework due tomorrow		
.	Read article for biology		
B	Start reading book for English due next week (chapters 1-3)		
.			
.			
.			
.			
.			
.			
C	Go to craft store to get art supplies to make signs for basketball game		
.	Look for new basketball shoes online		
.			
.			
.			
.			
.			

Figure 3.1

Example of a task list.

feel awkward, may be confusing, and may require effort to implement. That's ok! The more you practice, the easier it will become.

- Put all appointments, meetings, practices, and other commitments in the calendar and review the task list on a daily basis.
- Use and look at your task list and calendar *every day*!
- Select items from the master list to put on the daily task list.
- Rate each task as an "A," "B," or "C" task or assign numbers to tasks.
- Practice doing all of the "A" tasks before the "B" tasks and all of the "B" tasks before the "C" tasks or doing tasks in the order that you have set at the beginning of the day.
- Carry over tasks that are not completed from the previous day to the next day's list.

Figure 3.1 is an example of a task list. See if you like this format for your own task list, and, if so, feel free to base your task list on Worksheet 2: Task List, located in the Appendix. If this format doesn't work for you, you can develop your own, either on paper, digitally, or using an app.

CHAPTER 4

Session 4: What to Do When Things Aren't Getting Done: Breaking Down Tasks and Problem-Solving

OVERVIEW

The main skills that you will learn in this chapter are how to solve problems effectively and how to take a task that seems overwhelming at first and break it down into smaller, more manageable steps.

GOALS

- Continue to monitor your progress
- Review your use of the calendar and task list, particularly the "A," "B," "C" priority ratings
- Learn how to use problem-solving to overcome difficulties with finishing a task or choosing a solution to a problem
- Learn how to break down a large task into manageable steps
- Troubleshoot difficulties with breaking down large tasks into manageable steps
- Agree on home practice activities and anticipate difficulties using these techniques

Review of Symptom Checklist

As you have been doing each week, complete the ADHD symptom checklist that you and your therapist are using to track your symptoms. Be sure to review your score and take note of symptoms that have improved and those that are still problematic and share this information with your therapist.

Score: _____   **Date:** _____

Review of Medication Adherence

Using the ADHD Medication Form, record your prescribed dosage of medication and indicate the number of doses you actually took. Think about reasons for missed doses such as being distracted, running out of medication, your parents forgetting to give you your medication, or your thoughts about not wanting/needing to take medication. You should repeat this exercise at the beginning of every therapy session and share it with your therapist so that it can be discussed in therapy.

ADHD Medication Form

How many times were you supposed to take your ADHD medicine this week? _____

How many times did you actually take your ADHD medicine this week? _____

Reasons for missed doses: _____

_____

_____

Review of Previous Chapters

Each week you should examine your progress in using the skills that you have learned so far in this treatment. It is important to acknowledge the successes you have achieved and to problem-solve around any difficulties.

Review: Tools for Organization and Planning

- Use of calendar for managing appointments, practices, and other things that you need to do
- Use of task list system
- Use of priority rating system

Skill: Problem-Solving Strategies

This section involves learning to recognize when you are having difficulty completing a task or are becoming overwhelmed and cannot figure out exactly where to start. The reason we call problems "problems" is because there is no easy solution at hand. Usually any solution has pros and cons, and this typically can lead to issues such as procrastination. Once you recognize that there is a problem, you can use these problem-solving strategies to help.

We are going to go over two skills that may seem simple, but are actually quite powerful. The two skills are

1. Selecting an action plan, and
2. Breaking down an overwhelming task into smaller, more manageable steps.

Developing an action plan can be helpful when it is difficult to figure out a good solution to a problem or when there seem to be too many possible solutions and it feels overwhelming. Selecting an action plan involves the five steps that are listed next.

Skill: Five Steps in Problem-Solving

Use these instructions in conjunction with Worksheet 3: Problem-Solving: Selection of Action Plan, located in the Appendix:

1. *Articulate the problem*: Try to describe the problem in as few words as possible—one to two sentences at the most. Examples might be "I cannot decide whether I should switch out of my AP English class," "I cannot decide if I should take a gap year after I graduate from high school."

2. *List all possible solutions*: In these columns, try to figure out all the possible solutions—regardless of how realistic they are, what the consequences may be, or whether or not they sound outrageous. The idea is to generate a list of as many different solutions as possible.

3. *List the pros and cons of each solution*: Now is the time to realistically look at each solution. In these columns, try to figure out what you think would happen if you picked that solution. List the pros (advantages) and cons (disadvantages) of each.

4. *Rate each solution*: Using the final column, rate the pros and cons of the solution on a scale from 1 to 10, with 1 being a terrible solution and 10 being a great solution. Try to be as objective as possible, but also try to factor in how hard it would be to carry out this solution. For example, if one solution is to say "no" to something, you should factor in whether this will cause you anxiety as well as whether it will be likely to work.

5. *Implement the best option*: Now that you have rated each option on a scale of 1–10, review each rating. Look at the one that is rated the highest. Determine if this is really the solution that you would like to pick. If so, use the other skills you have learned in this treatment program (problem-solving, organizing, task list, calendar) to implement it.

Skill: Pick Three

Use these instructions with Worksheet 4: Problem-Solving: Pick Three, located in the Appendix.

If Worksheet 3: Problem-Solving: Selection of Action Plan, seems too complicated or overwhelming, you can use Worksheet 4: Problem-Solving: Pick Three, also located in the Appendix. The instructions are similar, but with fewer steps. For Worksheet 4, you first describe the problem and write it out on the first line. Then you generate three possible solutions and write them in the first column. Next, you write the pros and cons of each of the three solutions and give each solution a rating. Finally, you choose the best or "winning" solution.

Skill: Breaking Down Large Tasks into Manageable Steps

If a task seems overwhelming, we are much more likely to procrastinate and not even attempt to start working on it. Even if the solution is clear, it may just feel easier to put off working on the overwhelming task. By learning how to break down large tasks into smaller, more manageable steps, you will increase the likelihood that you will *start* (and therefore eventually complete) important tasks.

How to Break Down Large Tasks into Manageable Steps:

1. *Choose a difficult or complicated task* from your task list (or the solution that you identified as the best option on Worksheet 3 or 4 from the previous exercise).
2. *List the steps that you must complete.* You can do this using small note cards or plain paper, or you can type the steps into your phone, tablet, or computer. Ask questions such as, "What is the first thing that I would need to do to make this happen?"
3. *For each step, make sure that it is manageable.* Ask yourself, "Is this something that I could realistically complete in one day?" and "Is this something that I would want to put off doing?" If the step itself is overwhelming, then break that step into smaller steps. Don't be afraid to do this as many times as you need to so that you end up with tasks that you can easily complete in a single sitting.
4. *Add each individual step to your master list.*
5. *Individual steps can be moved to the daily task lists one at a time as needed*—just put the step or steps that you are hoping to complete on a particular day on the daily list for that day.
6. *Individual tasks can be placed on your calendar in specific time slots* if you find this helpful.

You can also consider using Worksheet 5: Problem-Solving: Small Steps, located in the Appendix.

Potential Pitfalls

You may find that distractibility interferes with your ability to use these skills. Don't worry! You will learn skills for coping with distractibility in the next module. It is important to focus on one set of skills at a time so that you can make progress. Try to focus on applying the organizational skills as best you can and don't worry about the issues that you have not learned to deal with yet.

Also, you may find that you have some difficulty figuring out how to rate the pros, cons, and overall solutions and deciding how many steps make sense for each task. Remember, each new skill will take lots of practice before it comes naturally to you. The most important thing is that you are trying to learn new skills so that you can be more effective and organized. Just keep trying! It will get easier as you get used to using the new skills.

Practice

As you are learning in this treatment, practicing new skills is vital so that you become familiar with them, are able to easily use the tools, and begin to see the positive results that can emerge when you consistently use these cognitive-behavioral therapy (CBT) strategies. Recognize that, at first, when you are learning a new skill, it may feel awkward, may be confusing, and may require effort to implement. That's ok! The more you practice, the easier it will become.

- Continue to put all your appointments in the calendar.
- Put all tasks on the master task list.
- Use and look at the task list and calendar *every day*!
- Use your priority ratings.
- Practice doing your tasks according to the priority ratings you have set.
- Carry over tasks that are not completed to the next day's daily task list.
- Practice using Worksheet 3: Problem-Solving: Selection of Action Plan or Worksheet 4: Problem-Solving: Pick Three for at least one item on the task list.
- Practice breaking down one large task from the task list into smaller steps.

CHAPTER 5

Session 5: How to Organize Everything

The main goal of this chapter is for you to learn strategies for developing systems to stay organized. You can develop a system to deal with school papers. You can also work on developing any other types of organizational systems that might be helpful for you, such as systems for computer files, emails, or things in your room.

For the school paper filing system, you will learn both how to *triage* (put in order of importance and organize) assignments as they come in and how to develop a filing system so that you can find important papers later when you need them. In addition, part of this session involves reviewing the organizational skills that you have learned so far in this module so that you will be ready to move on to the module on distractibility next week.

GOALS

- Continue to monitor your progress
- Review your use of the calendar and task list
- Review your use of priority ratings
- Review your use of problem-solving and breaking down large tasks into manageable steps
- Develop a sorting system for dealing with papers
- Develop a filing system for important papers

- Develop other organizational system/s that might be useful
- Agree on home practice activities and anticipate difficulties using these techniques

Review of Symptom Checklist

As you have been doing each week, complete the attention-deficit/hyperactivity disorder (ADHD) symptom checklist that you and your therapist are using to track your symptoms. Be sure to review your score and take note of symptoms that have improved and those that are still problematic and share this information with your therapist.

Score: _____   **Date:** _____

Review of Medication Adherence

Using the ADHD Medication Form, record your prescribed dosage of medication and indicate the number of doses you actually took. Think about reasons for missed doses such as being distracted, running out of medication, your parents forgetting to give you your medication, or your thoughts about not wanting/needing to take medication. You should repeat this exercise at the beginning of every therapy session and share it with your therapist so that it can be discussed in therapy.

ADHD Medication Form

How many times were you supposed to take your ADHD medicine this week? _____

How many times did you actually take your ADHD medicine this week? _____

Reasons for missed doses: _____

_____

_____

Each week you should examine your progress in implementing the skills that you have learned so far in this treatment. It is important to acknowledge the successes you have achieved and to problem-solve around any difficulties.

Review: Tools for Organization and Planning

- *Use of calendar for managing appointments*: At this point, you should discuss any problems that you are having with using your calendar system.
- *Use of task list system*: Review any difficulties that you are having with using your task list on a daily basis.
- *Use of the priority ratings*: If you are having any trouble with prioritizing tasks, this should be discussed at this point.
- *Use of problem-solving (selecting an action plan) and breaking down large tasks into small steps*: Consider your use of these strategies and practice one or both skills using examples from your current task list.

Skill: Developing Organizational Systems for Papers and Other Items

Most people find it somewhat difficult to organize school papers, mail, email, important papers, and electronic files. Individuals with ADHD can find it overwhelming to deal with these issues. This can lead to arguments with family members and misplacing important documents.

Putting a structured system in place can make this issue feel less overwhelming and easier to deal with.

In this session, you will be learning about organizational strategies. Using these strategies may feel unfamiliar and may take some additional time to use in the *short term*, but in the *long term*, these strategies will make organization much easier.

When you have an organizational system in place, it will decrease problems related to poor organization, such as feeling overwhelmed

---

or out of control and missing out on opportunities because of missed deadlines or lost paperwork.

Furthermore, many people find it difficult to throw things away, resulting in a cluttered environment which makes it even more difficult to find important papers or other items. We recommend coming up with organizational systems that are both simple and effective. If systems are too complicated, they end up being too-time consuming to use and people stop using them.

Before coming up with systems, you should figure out where you are having difficulties with organization—for example, email, homework papers, computer files, your bedroom, your backpack, or your locker at school can be common areas of difficulty. Think about the complications that may be caused by your organizational problems. These issues can often cause difficulties with parents or siblings. It is helpful to start with an area that is really upsetting for you. Look at Box 5.1 to help you come up with your own system.

Box 5.1 Developing an organizational system

1. *Decide where you will keep your important things.* (Don't spend too much time making this decision.)
2. *Pick one area or container to use.* Keep it simple! You only need to keep things here that you will *really* need.
3. *Set up your main files* (college applications, high school classes) or categories (school supplies, art supplies).
4. *For electronic documents—sort them into folders.* The easiest way to do it is to make one folder for each class you are taking, and then additional folders for other things.
5. *For emails—also sort these into folders* for different classes or activities (for example, one for English class, one for History . . . , and then one for, say, your sports team if your coach emails you, or your drama club if you are in one, and so on). Answer the email and then file it so that you don't have too many emails in your general inbox.
6. *Plan specific times each week that you will use the system.* Problem-solve to make sure that you are not choosing unrealistic times.
7. These tips are general, and it will be important for you and your therapist to discuss and make a plan for your specific needs.
8. Remember that it is important to practice these skills for long enough so that they become a habit. Don't give up too soon!!

Potential Pitfalls

One potential pitfall when trying to sort and organize things is thinking that everything is important. This is just not true. Discuss with people who are close to you what items or files really need to be saved. It is especially helpful to talk with people who have good organizational systems and don't seem to have a lot of clutter around, to get their perspective.

It may take some time in the short term to set up these systems, but it will be worth it in the long term! Try to use the strategies of problem-solving and breaking down large tasks into smaller steps if you feel overwhelmed by the prospect of setting up your organizational systems. If you take one step at a time, you will be able to complete these tasks.

You may need to discuss your proposed systems with your parents before you set them up. It will work much better if everyone is on the same page about where everything goes. For example, if your parents are moving your school papers into a pile on your desk, but you are trying to sort papers into bins for each class, it won't work very well.

Practice

As you are learning in this treatment, practicing new skills is vital so that you become familiar with them, are able to easily use the tools, and begin to see the positive results that can emerge when you consistently use these cognitive behavioral therapy (CBT) strategies. Recognize that, at first, when you are learning a new skill, it may feel awkward, may be confusing, and may require effort to implement. That's ok! The more you practice, the easier it will become.

- Continue to use the calendar every day to record appointments, practices, rehearsals, and other time commitments, and put homework and other tasks on the task list every day.
- Use and look at the task list and calendar *every day*!
- Use your priority ratings.
- Practice doing your tasks according to the priority ratings you have set.
- Carry over tasks that are not completed to the next day's task list.
- Practice using Worksheet 3: Problem-Solving: Selection of Action Plan, for at least one item on the task list.
- Practice breaking down one large task from the task list into smaller steps.
- Set up and use the organizational systems developed with your therapist in session.

How to Keep Going and Not Get Distracted

CHAPTER 6

Session 6: Figuring Out Your Attention Span and Learning How to Delay Distractions

OVERVIEW

The main goals of this chapter are for you to (1) figure out how long you can hold your attention when doing tasks you don't want to do and (2) start using the distractibility delay technique.

The distractibility delay involves timing your ability to stay focused on difficult activities and also reducing tasks into "chunks" that take approximately that length of time. You will also learn how to delay the time when you become distracted from the task at hand.

GOALS

- Continue to monitor your progress
- Review your use of the calendar, task list, and work from previous chapters
- Learn how to measure your attention span and develop a plan for breaking down tasks into steps that take that length of time
- Use the distractibility delay
- Agree on home practice activities and anticipate difficulties using these techniques

Review of Symptom Checklist

As you have been doing each week, complete the attention-deficit/hyper-activity disorder (ADHD) symptom checklist that you and your therapist are using to track your symptoms. Be sure to review your score and take note of symptoms that have improved and those that are still problematic and share this information with your therapist.

Score: _____   Date: _____

Review of Medication Adherence

Using the ADHD Medication Form, record your prescribed dosage of medication and indicate the number of doses you actually took. Think about reasons for missed doses such as being distracted, running out of medication, your parents forgetting to give you your medication, or your thoughts about not wanting/needing to take medication. You should repeat this exercise at the beginning of every therapy session and share it with your therapist so that it can be discussed in therapy.

ADHD Medication Form

How many times were you supposed to take your ADHD medicine this week? _____

How many times did you actually take your ADHD medicine this week? _____

Reasons for missed doses: _____

_____

_____

Review of Previous Chapters

Each week you should examine your progress in implementing the skills that you have learned so far in this treatment. It is important to acknowledge the successes you have achieved and to problem-solve around any difficulties.

Review: Tools for Organization and Planning

- *Use of calendar for managing your schedule*: At this point, you should discuss any problems that you are having with using your calendar system.
- *Use of task list system*: Review any difficulties that you are having with using your task list on a daily basis.
- *Use of priority ratings*: If you are having any trouble with prioritizing tasks, this should be discussed at this point.
- *Use of problem-solving (selecting an action plan) and breaking down large tasks into small steps*: Consider your use of these strategies and practice one or both skills using examples from your current task list.

Concepts of Attention Span and Distractibility

Individuals with ADHD often report that they are unable to complete tasks because other, less important tasks or distractions get in the way. Having a short attention span is part of ADHD. We do not view having a short attention span as being associated with intelligence or ability, but rather as representing a need for people with ADHD to use extra skills in order to do the things that they want and need to do.

There are many examples of people who can do extraordinary things despite having certain limitations. For example, the singer, Apl.de.ap from the Black-Eyed Peas has a visual impairment, and former president Bill Clinton has hearing loss. They needed to use extra coping skills to achieve excellence in their fields.

The goal of treatment is to help you become your best, most effective self. We will use several strategies to help you accomplish this goal.

Skill: Gauging Your Attention Span

There really is no such thing as an exact amount of time representing each individual's attention span. The amount of time that a person can work on a particular task depends on many factors, including those related to the task (how difficult or complex the task is) and those related to the individual (how tired you are, level of interest in the task, whether you have eaten recently, and so on). What you are trying to figure out with the following exercise is a reasonable amount of time that you can expect yourself to do something that is not very interesting to you. Often, individuals with ADHD will set unrealistic goals for themselves (for example, "I am going to study for 8 hours straight"), and then they end up not wanting to start the task because the goal is so overwhelming. There are two steps that you can take to set more realistic goals and make it more likely that you will make progress toward these goals.

1. The first step is to estimate the length of time that you can work on a boring or unattractive task without stopping.
2. The second step is to use the problem-solving skills that you learned earlier to break down a task into steps that last this length of time. For example, if you think that you can work on a boring task for 10 minutes, break down a larger task (for example, math homework) into 10-minute chunks.

Time It!

During the upcoming week, pick a task or activity that you know you have been avoiding. Find a way to time yourself while working on the task, either using a watch or the stopwatch function on your computer or phone.

- Figure out a time when you can work on a task that you may find boring, difficult, or that you have been avoiding.
- Start timing yourself.
- Begin working.
- Keep going as long as you normally would before taking a break, going to the bathroom, or stopping the activity because you have gotten up or started doing something different.
- When the urge comes to stop working, record the time.

Repeat this exercise a couple of times. Average out the amount of time that it took before you became distracted and make this your starting attention span time.

Now—the trick is to use the problem-solving skills learned earlier to break down overwhelming or boring activities or tasks into chunks that take approximately the amount of time that you can hold your attention. We recommend only taking breaks in between the chunks.

As you do this more and more often, try to increase the length of time that you are able to focus on boring or unattractive tasks.

It is important not only to schedule specific times to work, but also to schedule in breaks. You should time both the work time blocks and the breaks so that you don't end up taking breaks that are too long. For example, it will take a long time to finish a task if you work for 30 minutes and then take a 3-hour break.

Skill: Distractibility Delay[1]

When you are working on a boring task, it is inevitable that distractions will pop into your head from time to time and serve as big temptations! Often, the distractions seem to grow in importance as time goes on. The difficult problem here is the following question: Is it really that these distractions are important or is it that they *become* more important because:

1. They represent something different and therefore more interesting.
2. The task you set out to do now is not attractive.

Is It More Important or Just More Attractive?

A good example of this question relates to one of our clients, Amy, who was working on a long essay for one of her classes. She told us that whenever she sat down to do her work, she would feel the need to clean her room. Amy did not like cleaning, but she would have the urge to clean whenever she needed to write. In fact, she got to the point where she felt that she just could not work unless her room was totally clean! Over the years, we have found that other clients who were in school would report similar stories. In these cases, cleaning becomes a distraction that grows in importance. Even though it is typically not an attractive or important task, it becomes much more attractive than the task at hand, which feels overwhelming.

Once you have determined the length of time for which you can hold your attention and you have broken down tasks into steps that take about that amount of time, the next step is to try to build skills to delay distractions.

Distractibility Delay

The *distractibility delay* is an exercise that can be done in addition to the strategies just described. It is similar to an exercise used in anxiety disorder treatments and can be used as a strategy for delaying paying attention to distractions while working on boring or unattractive tasks. Clients with ADHD often report that thoughts pop into their heads while they are working on a task. They say that it is tempting to simply stop working on their current task and shift their attention to the distraction. They report that this is because they worry about forgetting the distraction (like remembering to feed the cat) and not doing what they need to do. The reality is that this has been their experience in the past, but it is possible to both take care of the distracting tasks and finish the task at hand. Thus, the distractibility delay can be described as a tool (1) for getting the distractions out of your head and (2) for getting you to focus on the task at hand. Over time, you will gain confidence that these thoughts will not be forgotten and will actually get done.

You should have a piece of paper or a note app open in your phone or other device when starting work on a boring or unattractive task. Then set a timer (you can use your phone for this as well) for the agreed-upon length of time (for example, 30 minutes). When a distraction comes into your head, write down the distracting thought on the piece of paper or type it into the note on your phone, but *do not* take action on the distraction. Instead, return to the task that you are working on. When the timer goes off, look at the list and decide if any of the distracting tasks actually need to be completed right away. If so, you can complete that task immediately.

You should repeat this process until the task is completed (or the portion of the task that you have set out to do for the day). You can then review the list of distractions and decide if (1) they need to be completed right away, (2) they should be added to your master or daily task list, or (3) they are unimportant tasks that do not need to be completed. The piece of paper should then be thrown away (or the electronic note should be deleted) at the end of the exercise so that you do not end up with multiple lists.

You can use coping statements to help you return to the task at hand. These can include, "I will worry about this later," "This is not a high-priority task," or "I will come back to this when the timer goes off."

You can use the distractibility delay in a similar fashion during classes. For example, if you have difficulties with impulsively blurting out comments or questions, bring a notepad or tablet to class where you can write down a cue word or phrase and then try to refocus your attention on what the teacher is saying. When there is a break in the class discussion, bring up your question or comment.

Steps for Distractibility Delay

1. Put a piece of scrap paper or your phone with a blank, open note next to you.
2. Set your timer for a specific length of time—this should be the length of time for which you can usually hold your attention.
3. Start working on a task.
4. When a distraction pops into your head, write it down on your scrap paper or on your electronic note, but *don't do anything about it* (for example, don't get up and start making a phone call, putting something away, feeding the cat, working on homework for a different class, and so on).
5. Once the distraction has been written down, use coping statements such as, "I will worry about it later," or "This is not a high-priority task," or "I will come back to this when the timer goes off."
6. Return to the original task until you are finished with the "chunk of time" that you have selected.
7. When the timer goes off, take a break. At this point, look at your distraction list and decide if the tasks really need to be done immediately.
8. When done working for the day, go back to the distraction list. Decide if these are actually important items or if they are things that only became attractive because they were not the task you were working on.
9. If they are in fact important, either do them or add them to your task list.

---

[1] The distractibility delay technique was inspired by a similar technique used in treatment of generalized anxiety disorder, articulated by Craske & Barlow (2006).

Potential Pitfalls

These skills may seem simple, but they aren't! Don't expect that you will be able to use them effectively right away. The extra coping skills that you are learning to help you overcome your short attention span and distractibility may take some time to develop. Remember, it took you many years to develop your current habits, and it will take some time to develop more effective habits. Stick with this program; it will be worth it in the long run!

Practice

As you are learning in this treatment, practicing new skills is vital so that you become familiar with them, are able to easily use the tools, and begin to see the positive results that can emerge when you consistently use these cognitive behavioral therapy (CBT) strategies. Recognize that, at first, when you are learning a new skill, it may feel awkward, may be confusing, and may require effort to implement. That's ok! The more you practice, the easier it will become.

- Continue to use the calendar every day to keep track of your schedule, and put homework and other tasks on the task list every day.
- Use and look at the task list and calendar *every day*!
- Use your priority ratings.
- Practice doing your tasks according to the priority ratings you have set.
- Carry over tasks that are not completed to the next day's task list.
- Practice using Worksheet 3: Problem-Solving: Selection of Action Plan or Worksheet 4: Problem-Solving: Pick Three for at least one item on the task list.
- Practice breaking down one large task from the task list into smaller steps.
- Use the organizational systems developed in this program.
- Measure attention span.
- Use the distractibility delay when working on boring or unattractive tasks.

CHAPTER 7 — Session 7: Optimize Your Setting

OVERVIEW

The main goals of this chapter are for you to (1) learn how to modify your environment to reduce distractibility and (2) learn how to create "reminders" for yourself to focus on the task at hand.

You will learn how to reduce the number of distractions in your environment and create a situation that will set the stage for you to be able to concentrate. You will also learn a strategy to help you check in with yourself to see if you are distracted. This strategy will enable you to refocus on the task at hand if you have become distracted.

GOALS

- Continue to monitor your progress
- Review your continual use of skills from previous chapters
- Continue breaking down tasks into steps that match the length of your attention span and continue using the distractibility delay
- Learn how to reduce the number of things that are likely to distract you in your environment
- Learn how to check in with yourself to see if you are distracted, and learn how to refocus on the task at hand when you do become distracted

■ Agree on home practice activities and anticipate difficulties using these techniques

Review of Symptom Checklist

As you have been doing each week, complete the attention-deficit/hyperactivity disorder (ADHD) symptom checklist that you and your therapist are using to track your symptoms. Be sure to review your score and take note of symptoms that have improved and those that are still problematic and share this information with your therapist.

Score: _____   **Date:** _____

Review of Medication Adherence

Using the ADHD Medication Form, record your prescribed dosage of medication and indicate the number of doses you actually took. Think about reasons for missed doses such as being distracted, running out of medication, your parents forgetting to give you your medication, or your thoughts about not wanting/needing to take medication. You should repeat this exercise at the beginning of every therapy session and share it with your therapist so that it can be discussed in therapy.

ADHD Medication Form

How many times were you supposed to take your ADHD medicine this week? _____

How many times did you actually take your ADHD medicine this week? _____

Reasons for missed doses: _____

_____

_____

Each week you should examine your progress in implementing the skills that you have learned so far in this treatment. It is important to acknowledge the successes you have achieved and to problem-solve around any difficulties.

Review: Tools for Organization and Planning

- *Use of calendar for managing your schedule*: At this point, you should discuss any problems that you are having with using your calendar system.
- *Use of task list system*: Review any difficulties that you are having with using your task list on a daily basis.
- *Use of priority ratings*: If you are having any trouble with prioritizing tasks, this should be discussed at this point.
- *Use of problem-solving (selecting an action plan) and breaking down large tasks into small steps*: Consider your use of these strategies, and practice one or both skills using examples from your current task list.

Review: Tools for Reducing Distractibility

- *Use of the strategy of breaking down tasks into manageable chunks*: At this point, you should discuss with your therapist any problems that you are having with breaking down tasks.
- *Use of the distractibility delay*: Review any difficulties that you are having with the distractibility delay technique.

Skill: Controlling Your Homework Environment

It is important for individuals with ADHD to do homework in an environment that has few distractions. Even with the distractibility coping skills discussed in the previous chapter, most people are somewhat distractible when they are trying to concentrate. Sometimes, distractions interfere to the point where it is too difficult to get anything done.

At this time, think about the environment in which you try to do your homework. Ask yourself, "What are the things that typically distract me from my homework?" Some typical distractions include:

- The telephone ringing or a notification popping up on your phone, computer, or tablet
- Surfing the internet, playing games, using social media
- Replying to e-mails or texts
- Noticing other things on the desk or table that need attention
- Listening to music
- Watching a show
- Speaking to a friend or family member who is in the room
- Looking at something going on outside the window

What are the types of things that typically get in the way when you are trying to get a project done? For each item that is distracting to you, come up with a strategy that reduces this distraction. For example, you can:

- Silence your phone or put it on vibrate
- Move your phone to a different room
- Close your web browser and/or e-mail
- Block sites like Facebook, Twitter, and Instagram from your web browser temporarily
- Turn off alerts on your phone, computer, or tablet
- Clear off your desk or workspace
- Turn off music or shows
- Change background noise or music to white noise or music without lyrics
- Ask others not to disturb you because you are working
- Turn your desk away from the window or other distractions

Use Worksheet 6: Strategies for Reducing Distractions, located in the Appendix, to identify and eliminate usual distractions from your homework environment.

Location, location, location!
We recommend finding one place in your house where you can do important tasks without distraction. This should be a place that you are able to keep clutter-free. It could be your desk, it could be a table near your desk, or it could be any other "work space." Many people report that their desk becomes cluttered and is difficult to keep clean.

Of course, you can use your organizational systems discussed earlier in the treatment program. However, if you think that having a messy desk may not change, the idea here is to find another space that you can use that you do keep clear and have this be your work space. You want to set the stage for success—by setting up a work space that will allow you to be as productive as possible.

Interestingly, some people with ADHD report that they do not concentrate as well when they are in a totally silent environment. It may be helpful for you to try to figure out the circumstances that allow you to concentrate best. For example, many clients report that they concentrate better when there is a certain type of music playing in the background (often music that does not have lyrics that might be distracting).

Skill: Keeping Track of Important Objects

One hallmark of ADHD is losing things. This causes problems because it can cause you to be late for events and increase feelings of frustration.

At this point, take a moment to think of any difficulties that you experience with keeping track of important objects, such as your backpack, computer, school ID, house keys, wallet, or phone. Some of these may be items that you need to take with you whenever you leave the house.

The next step is to think of a specific place where you would like to keep these items. Some people will place a basket somewhere near the door and put the important items in the basket each time that they come in the door. You might want to have a specific spot where you charge things overnight, and you know always to grab your phone, tablet, computer, and/or watch from that spot before you leave for the day. The goal is to try to never put your phone or any of the other important items in any location except for the target location. The other important (and sometimes difficult) part of this skill is that any time you see one of these items out of place, you *must* immediately return it to the target location. You and your therapist might want to bring your parents into this discussion. If you think of a solution that would work for you, you might want to ask your parents to buy a basket, bin, cubby, or other storage unit that you can use to store your important things. You can improve the likelihood of success by making sure that everyone in the family is aware of the plan so that they can be on the same page and support your plan (for example, your sister can let you know if she sees your computer in the basement or your phone in the pantry, and you can put them back where they belong).

Having specific places where the important items belong increases the likelihood that you will be able to locate these items when you need them. You need to work to develop the habit.

Skill: Using Reminders

Imagine that you could have someone follow you around and constantly remind you about all of the skills that we have discussed. Having this person around would probably really increase your use of the skills. You would never forget. These skills require that you actively remember to do them. (Although, with practice, these will become habits that you eventually don't have to actively remember.)

For most people, having a 24-hour personal assistant is not possible, and we therefore recommend the use of reminders.

An alarm can be helpful in getting you to check in with yourself on a regular basis about whether or not you are doing what you are supposed to be doing. You can use an alarm clock, or an alarm on your watch, computer, or cell phone.

Set the alarm to go off at regularly scheduled intervals during time periods when you are trying to concentrate on a task. We recommend trying to have the alarm sound each half-hour—especially when you are trying to be productive.

When the alarm sounds, ask yourself, "Am I doing what I am supposed to be doing or did I get distracted?" If you notice that you have become distracted, immediately return to the task at hand.

Potential Pitfalls

It is easy to get frustrated with these strategies if they don't work right away. Remember, you are trying to develop new work habits. It takes lots of practice before new habits become second nature. Don't give up! Even if it seems like these skills don't work at first, keep at them. This will pay off in the long run when you are able to be less susceptible to distractions and get more accomplished.

Practice

As you are learning in this treatment, practicing new skills is vital so that you become familiar with them, are able to easily use the tools, and begin to see the positive results that can emerge when you consistently use these cognitive behavioral therapy (CBT) strategies. Recognize that, at first, when you are learning a new skill, it may feel awkward, may be confusing, and may require effort to implement. That's ok! The more you practice, the easier it will become.

- Continue to use the calendar every day to keep track of your schedule and put new tasks on the task list every day.
- Use and look at the task list and calendar *every day*!
- Use your priority ratings.
- Practice doing your tasks according to the priority ratings you have set.
- Carry over tasks that are not completed to the next day's task list.
- Practice using Worksheet 3: Problem-Solving: Selection of Action Plan or Worksheet 4: Problem-Solving: Pick Three for at least one item on the task list.
- Practice breaking down one large task from the task list into smaller steps.
- Use the organizational systems developed in this program.
- Use the distractibility delay when working on boring or unattractive tasks.
- Use your skills to reduce distraction in your homework environment.
- Start putting important items in specific places.
- Use reminders to check in with yourself to see if you have become distracted when you are trying to focus on completing a task.

How to Coach Yourself Better

CHAPTER 8

Session 8: Thinking, Feeling, and Acting

OVERVIEW

By now, you have developed systems for organizing, planning, and problem-solving, and you have been practicing skills for managing distractibility. The next section, targeting adaptive (effective or helpful) thinking, will help you increase your awareness of negative thoughts that can cause stress and mood problems and that can interfere with completing tasks.

This method of training yourself to think adaptively has been used in similar cognitive behavioral treatments and has been effective in treating many other psychological disorders, such as depression and anxiety disorders. This method of implementing and teaching cognitive-restructuring skills is based on the work of several other researchers using cognitive behavioral therapy (CBT) to work with people who have attention-deficit/hyperactivity disorder (ADHD), social phobia, and panic disorders. The major goal of learning to think about tasks and situations adaptively is to reduce the times when negative or ineffective thoughts or moods interfere with tasks and follow-through, cause distress, or make it more likely that you will get distracted.

Adaptive thinking will enable you to:

- Increase your awareness of negative, interfering thoughts;
- Develop strategies for keeping your thoughts in check; and
- Minimize symptoms

- Continue to monitor your progress
- Review your continual use of skills from previous chapters
- Learn basic principles of the cognitive model of mood
- Become skilled in identifying and labeling unhelpful automatic thoughts
- Agree on home practice activities and anticipate difficulties using these techniques

Review of Symptom Checklist

As you have been doing each week, complete the ADHD symptom checklist that you and your therapist are using to track your symptoms. Be sure to review your score and take note of symptoms that have improved and those that are still problematic and share this information with your therapist.

Score: _____   Date: _____

Review of Medication Adherence

Using the ADHD Medication Form, record your prescribed dosage of medication and indicate the number of doses you actually took. Think about reasons for missed doses such as being distracted, running out of medication, your parents forgetting to give you your medication, or your thoughts about not wanting/needing to take medication. You should repeat this exercise at the beginning of every therapy session and share it with your therapist so that it can be discussed in therapy.

```
┌─────────────────────────────────────────────────────────────────┐
│                      ADHD Medication Form                         │
│                                                                   │
│  How many times were you supposed to take your ADHD medicine      │
│  this week? _____                                     │
│                                                                   │
│                                                                   │
│  How many times did you actually take your ADHD medicine this     │
│  week? _____                                            │
│                                                                   │
│                                                                   │
│  Reasons for missed doses: _____ │
│                                                                   │
│  _____ │
│                                                                   │
│  _____ │
└─────────────────────────────────────────────────────────────────┘
```

Review of Previous Chapters

Each week you should review your progress in implementing skills from each of the previous chapters. It is important to acknowledge the successes you have achieved and to problem-solve around any difficulties.

Review: Tools for Organization and Planning

- *Use of calendar for managing schedule*: At this point, you should discuss any problems that you are having with using your calendar system.
- *Use of task list system*: Review any difficulties that you are having with using your task list on a daily basis.
- *Use of priority ratings*: If you are having any trouble with prioritizing tasks, this should be discussed at this point.
- *Use of problem-solving (selecting an action plan) and breaking down large tasks into small steps*: Consider your use of these strategies and practice one or both skills using examples from your current task list.

Review: Tools for Reducing Distractibility

- *Use of the strategy of breaking down tasks into manageable chunks*: At this point, you should discuss with your therapist any problems that you are having with breaking down tasks.
- *Use of the distractibility delay*: Review any difficulties that you are having with the distractibility delay technique.
- *Use of strategy to remove distractions from the environment.*
- *Use of strategy to have a specific place* for each important object.
- *Use of reminders or an alarm*: "Am I doing what I am supposed to be doing?"

The Cognitive Behavioral Model

Adaptive thinking is just what it sounds like. It is a way of thinking about situations in a manner that is adaptive or effective. Sometimes individuals have thoughts that are either inaccurate or unhelpful, and this can cause difficulties. By learning adaptive thinking, we are able to learn to challenge our inaccurate or unhelpful thoughts and come up with more effective or helpful ways of looking at situations. Adaptive thinking is important because of the relationship between thoughts, feelings, and behaviors, as illustrated in Figure 8.1.

This model emphasizes the important connection between your thoughts, feelings (emotions), and behaviors in a given situation. The cognitive part of CBT involves the way in which thoughts contribute to how people act and the way that thoughts contribute to how people feel.

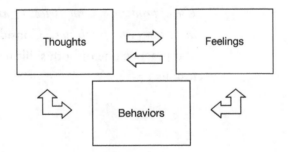

Figure 8.1

Basic cognitive behavioral model.

Every day, many different thoughts go through our minds. What is surprising is that often we are not particularly aware of these thoughts. However, they play an important role in determining how we are feeling in a situation and how we may respond. When we are feeling overwhelmed, stressed, or worried about completing a task, the thoughts that go through our minds play a very important role in determining what ends up happening.

These thoughts are "automatic" in that they happen on their own. For example, think about when you first learned to ride a bike. In order to coordinate many tasks at once, you had to be conscious of where your hands were placed on the handle bars, remember to look both ways before turns, ride in a straight line, and watch out for other traffic. You were doing many tasks at the same time that required your total attention.

Now, think about riding a bike today. You probably know how to ride without actively thinking about what you are doing. You likely don't even remember thinking about all of these steps because they have become automatic. This can be a positive thing in that it frees up your attention to focus on other things, like what you will do when you get to where you are going or what homework you need to do later on. However, if the thoughts are negative in tone, this can be problematic.

Less Helpful Automatic Thinking

In many situations, like the one we just discussed, automatic thoughts enable us to complete a task more easily. Unfortunately, in other situations, automatic thoughts interfere with achieving goals. For example, imagine you have to do a task that you will probably not enjoy, such as preparing for a big exam or writing a term paper. Imagine the following types of thoughts going through your mind:

"I am careless and am going to do this wrong."

"This is going to take forever."

"I'm probably going to fail this test."

"I will never get all of my homework finished."

"I am an idiot."

"I am going to be embarrassed in front of everyone for not doing this right."

If thoughts like these are going through your head, you can easily see that this task will feel overwhelming and stressful. This will increase the chance that you will procrastinate by doing any other possible task.

Relationship of Thoughts to Feelings and Behaviors

The behavior in this cycle is often some form of *avoidance*. Negative thoughts about a situation make a person avoid the situation because they (1) feel bad and (2) expect that the situation will not turn out well. Avoidance can lead to more anxiety, restlessness, and perhaps irritability or depression—the task doesn't get done, and then the person feels worse about it. Anxiety and depression may lead to more negative thinking, and around and around the cycle goes, making the problem worse and worse. For people with ADHD, this cycle worsens other symptoms such as inattention, procrastination, frustration, and depression.

The first step in breaking this cycle is to identify and slow down negative or ineffective automatic thinking. Becoming more aware of situations when negative thoughts occur is the first step in learning to think in more adaptive ways.

Thinking That Is Too Positive

So far, we have talked about *negative* automatic thoughts. However, researchers are now identifying another problematic way of thinking in individuals with ADHD that involves *overly optimistic thinking*. The idea is that people with ADHD often set overly optimistic goals and verbalize overly positive thoughts. This pattern can cause difficulties in that individuals feel good in the moment (for example, "I don't really need to do this today because I have plenty of time to do it next weekend"). However, this causes problems when the thinking and goal-setting are unrealistic and the person ends up failing to meet their goals. Thus, we will be working to *identify overly positive thoughts* in addition to helping you *identify negative thoughts*.

Skill: Identifying Negative/Unhelpful Automatic Thoughts

The *thought record* is a tool that was developed to help you learn how to identify, slow down, and restructure negative and/or unhelpful automatic thoughts. You can use the thought records provided in the Appendix, or you can write this information in your phone, on your computer, or on your tablet. There are several apps and web sites that allow you to enter this information, if you prefer.

Let's start with an upsetting situation that came up in the past week. Think about the past week and see if you can identify a time when you felt overwhelmed, stressed, sad, or upset.

Learning to complete a thought record (such as the one shown on Worksheet 7: Three-Column Thought Record, located in the Appendix) is best done with the aid of your therapist. We recommend practicing it over several sessions.

Column 1 should contain a brief description of the *situation*. When did it take place, where were you, with whom, what was going on, and so on? Ideally, the description of the situation should just be a sentence or two at most.

Column 2 should contain your *thoughts*. What was going through your mind at the time? What were you saying to yourself about the situation, about other people, and about your role in the situation? What were you afraid might happen? What is the worst thing that could happen if this feared outcome occurred? If another person is involved, what does this mean about how the other person feels/thinks about you?

When coming up with automatic thoughts, it is important to separate *thoughts* from *feelings*. Thoughts are what you think of the situation. Feelings go in the next column.

Column 3 should be a list of the *moods* or emotions you experienced (you may list several different feelings), and then rate the *intensity* of each feeling on a scale of 0–100 (with 0 = the least intense and 100 = the most intense). Examples of moods include angry, upset, happy, sad, depressed, anxious, and surprised.

Figure 8.2 is an example of a completed three-column thought record. Using Worksheet 7 in the Appendix, please complete a thought record using your own examples.

Time and Situation	Automatic Thoughts	Mood and Intensity
Writing an English paper.	I have to write the entire paper today.	Overwhelmed (80)
	I must do this perfectly.	Anxious (75)
	If I don't finish, my teacher will be upset.	Depressed (60)
	If the paper is not perfect, I will fail out of school and I won't be able to get into college.	Anxious (95)
	Actually, I don't need to start the paper today because I can do it on Sunday night.	Relieved (100)

Figure 8.2

Sample completed three-column thought record.

Introduction to Thinking Errors

Now that you see how certain situations can trigger automatic thoughts and negative (or at times positive) feelings, let's look more closely at the nature of these automatic thoughts. In our experience, and in the work of other cognitive behavioral therapists, common types of negative automatic thoughts often emerge. You can begin to see how these types of thoughts may interfere with your ability to complete tasks and also contribute to feeling depressed, anxious, or frustrated.

Listed here are some *common thinking traps*. These thinking errors are called "traps" because people tend to fall into them and get stuck. You should review each one to make sure you understand them all, and then begin to look for patterns to determine which types of errors may be especially problematic for you.

Common Thinking Traps

- *All or nothing thinking*: You see things in black-and-white categories. For example, *all* aspects of a project need to be completed immediately, or, if your performance falls short of perfect, you see it as a total failure.
- *Overgeneralization*: You see a single negative event as a never-ending pattern (it will continue to happen every time you do this activity).

- *Mental filter*: You pick out a single negative detail and dwell on it exclusively, overlooking other positive aspects of the situation. For example, if you got 5 questions wrong on an exam, even though you got 20 right, you focus on the questions you got wrong.
- *Disqualifying the positive*: You reject positive experiences by insisting that they "don't count" for some reason or other. In this way, you can maintain a negative belief that is contradicted by your everyday experiences.
- *Jumping to conclusions*: You make a negative interpretation, even though there are no definite facts that convincingly support your conclusion.
  - *Mind reading*: You conclude that someone is reacting negatively to you or doesn't like you, and you don't bother to check this out.
  - *Fortune telling*: You anticipate that things will turn out badly, and you feel that your prediction is a predetermined fact.
- *Magnification/Minimization*: You exaggerate the importance of things (such as your mistake or someone else's achievement), or you inappropriately shrink things until they appear tiny (your own desirable qualities or other people's imperfections).
- *Catastrophizing*: You attribute extreme and horrible consequences to the outcomes of events. For example, one mistake at work means being fired from your job.
- *Emotional reasoning*: You assume that your negative emotions necessarily reflect the way things really are: "I feel it, so it must be true."
- *"Should" statements*: You try to motivate yourself with "shoulds" and "shouldn'ts," as if you need to be punished before you could be expected to do anything. When directed toward others, you feel anger, frustration, and resentment.
- *Labeling and mislabeling*: This is an extreme form of overgeneralization. Instead of describing an error, you attach a negative label to yourself or others. An example of this would be calling yourself a "loser" or a "jerk."
- *Personalization*: You see negative events as indicative of some negative characteristic of yourself or others, or you take responsibility for events that were not your doing.
- *Maladaptive thinking*: You focus on a thought that may be true but over which you have no control. Excessively thinking about it can be self-critical or can distract you from an important task or from attempting new behaviors.

- *Overly optimistic thinking*: You think about a situation in an overly optimistic way that feels good in the moment but leads to procrastination and/or avoidance and is not effective in the long run. For example, you decide not to start working on your project today because you tell yourself that you will definitely have time to do it on the weekend.

Skill: Labeling Thinking Traps

Now that you have learned about common types of thinking traps, let's go back to the thought record you filled out earlier (Worksheet 7). For each of the automatic thoughts you listed, rewrite them on Worksheet 8: Four-Column Thought Record (in the Appendix) and review the list of thinking traps to see if you can identify these common patterns in your thinking. Then, list the appropriate thinking trap in Column 4 of Worksheet 8.

It's important to understand that not all negative thoughts represent thinking errors. Sometimes it is realistic that a situation produces a negative thought, which in turn contributes to a negative feeling. For example, imagine that you had been studying for an exam for many days and you were driving to school to take the exam. Then, suddenly you encountered a traffic jam due to a car accident that occurred earlier. Now, if your thought was, "Oh no. . . . I hope I won't be late. I studied so hard for this exam," and you were feeling anxious and perhaps frustrated, that would make sense! The challenge for you would be to *problem-solve*—in other words to try to stay calm, perhaps call the instructor to let her know that you are going to be late, and to focus on driving safely.

However, if, in addition to those thoughts, you also said to yourself, "Bad things always happen to me, I can never do anything right, I am going to miss the exam and fail the class," we can imagine that your anxiety and despair would intensify and that you may be more likely to drive dangerously. Furthermore, if you did get to the exam in time, you most likely would not be able to concentrate as well as you did when you were studying. Looking closely, you can see that these thoughts, respectively, could be classified as *overgeneralization*, *personalization*, and *jumping to conclusions*. Look at Figure 8.3, which is an example of a completed four-column thought record.

Time and Situation	Automatic Thoughts	Mood and Intensity	Thinking Trap
Writing an English paper.	I have to write the entire paper today.	Overwhelmed (80)	All or nothing thinking
	I must do this perfectly.	Anxious (75)	All or nothing thinking
	If I don't finish, my teacher will be upset.	Depressed (60)	Jumping to conclusions (mind reading)
	If the paper is not perfect, I will fail out of school and I won't be able to get into college.	Anxious (95)	Jumping to conclusions (fortune telling), Catastrophizing
	Actually, I don't need to start the paper today because I can do it on Sunday night.	Relieved (100)	Overly Optimistic Thinking

Figure 8.3

Sample completed four-column thought record.

Potential Pitfalls

For some people, writing out negative thoughts makes the thoughts "seem more real" or more difficult to cope with. Because of this, they are reluctant to complete thought records. However, the thought is in your mind, interfering, regardless of whether or not you write it down. Completing the thought record will actually help you feel better about the situation, despite the initial difficulty of seeing your thought written out on paper or electronically.

You may find that it is hard to label your feeling(s) and may think that you have to come up with the perfect emotion to describe your feelings. In actuality, this is not true. Use the first word that comes to mind, even if it is not perfect. Over time, it will become easier to label your feelings.

Preliminary Instructions for Adaptive Thinking

The purpose of using thought records is to identify and modify negative, automatic thoughts in situations that lead to feeling overwhelmed.

The first step in learning to think in more useful ways is to become more aware of these thoughts and their relationship to your feelings. If you are anticipating a stressful situation or a task that is making you feel overwhelmed, write out your thoughts about this situation.

If a situation has already passed and you find that you are thinking about it negatively or if, after the fact, you realize that you were having unhelpful thoughts, list your thoughts for this situation.

- The *first column* is a description of the situation.
- The *second column* is for you to list your thoughts during a stressful, overwhelming, or uncontrollable situation.
- The *third column* is for you to write down what emotions or feelings you are having when thinking these thoughts (for example, depressed, sad, angry).
- The *fourth column* is for you to see if your thoughts match the list of "thinking traps." These may include:
    - *All or nothing thinking*
    - *Overgeneralization*
    - *Mental filter*
    - *Disqualifying the positive*
    - *Jumping to conclusions*
        - *Mind reading*
        - *Fortune telling*
    - *Magnification/Minimization*
    - *Catastrophizing*
    - *Emotional reasoning*
    - *"Should" statements*
    - *Labeling and mislabeling*
    - *Personalization*
    - *Maladaptive thinking*
    - *Overly optimistic thinking*

In this session, try to anticipate which situations you may want to work on in the upcoming week. In addition, be sure to anticipate any problems that may get in the way of completing the exercises. For example, having a busy schedule, going out of town for a sports tournament, or not knowing how to complete an assignment may make it more difficult to practice your skills. We have found that if you can anticipate and problem-solve in advance, these obstacles can become manageable, and you will be more likely to achieve success with the new skills. Remember that you do not have to complete these home assignments perfectly! The idea is to begin monitoring your thoughts that arise in difficult situations and begin practicing identifying the common types of thinking errors.

Practice

As you are learning in this treatment, practicing new skills is vital so that you become familiar with them, are able to easily use the tools, and begin to see the positive results that can emerge when you consistently use these CBT strategies. Recognize that, at first, when you are learning a new skill, it may feel awkward, may be confusing, and may require effort to implement. That's ok! The more you practice, the easier it will become.

- Continue to use the calendar every day to keep track of your schedule and put new tasks on the task list every day.
- Use and look at the task list and calendar *every day*!
- Use your priority ratings.
- Practice doing your tasks according to the priority ratings.
- Carry over tasks that are not completed to the next day's task list.
- Practice using Worksheet 3: Problem-Solving: Selection of Action Plan or Worksheet 4: Problem-Solving: Pick Three for at least one item on the task list.
- Practice breaking down one large task from the task list into smaller steps.
- Use the organizational systems developed in this program.
- Use the distractibility delay when working on boring or unattractive tasks.
- Use your skills to reduce distraction in your homework environment.
- Start putting important items in specific places.
- Use reminders to check in with yourself to see if you have become distracted when you are trying to focus on completing a task.
- Read the "Preliminary Instructions for Adaptive Thinking" earlier in this chapter to learn about completing a thought record.
- Write out examples of thoughts on Worksheet 8 for at least two situations during the week.

The primary goal of this chapter is for you to learn how to develop alternate thoughts to replace your negative and/or unhelpful thoughts. You will do this by working through a process called *cognitive restructuring*, which involves observing your thoughts, identifying the thoughts that are inaccurate or unhelpful, and then coming up with alternate thoughts that are more accurate or helpful.

- Continue to monitor your progress
- Review your continual use of skills from previous chapters
- Review thought records completed at home
- Discuss coaching styles and coaching story
- Learn how to come up with alternative thoughts
- Agree on home practice activities and anticipate difficulties using these techniques

Review of Symptom Checklist

As you have been doing each week, complete the attention-deficit/hyperactivity disorder (ADHD) symptom checklist that you and your therapist are using to track your symptoms. Be sure to review your score and take note of symptoms that have improved and those that are still problematic and share this information with your therapist.

Score: _____   **Date:** _____

Review of Medication Adherence

Using the ADHD Medication Form, record your prescribed dosage of medication and indicate the number of doses you actually took. Think about reasons for missed doses such as being distracted, running out of medication, your parents forgetting to give you your medication, or your thoughts about not wanting/needing to take medication. You should repeat this exercise at the beginning of every therapy session and share it with your therapist so that it can be discussed in therapy.

ADHD Medication Form

How many times were you supposed to take your ADHD medicine this week? _____

How many times did you actually take your ADHD medicine this week? _____

Reasons for missed doses: _____

_____

_____

Review of Previous Chapters

Each week you should review your progress implementing skills from each of the previous chapters. It is important to acknowledge the successes you have achieved and to problem-solve around any difficulties.

Review: Tools for Organization and Planning

- *Use of calendar for managing your schedule*: At this point, you should discuss any problems that you are having with using your calendar system.
- *Use of task list system*: Review any difficulties that you are having with using your task list on a daily basis.
- *Use of priority ratings*: If you are having any trouble with prioritizing tasks, this should be discussed at this point.
- *Use of problem-solving (selecting an action plan) and breaking down large tasks into small steps*: Consider your use of these strategies and practice one or both skills using examples from your current task list.

Review: Tools for Reducing Distractibility

- *Use of the strategy of breaking down tasks into manageable chunks*: At this point, you should discuss with your therapist any problems that you are having with breaking down tasks.
- *Use of the distractibility delay*: Review any difficulties that you are having with the distractibility delay technique.
- *Use of strategy to remove distractions from the environment.*
- *Use of strategy to have a specific place* for each important object.
- *Use of reminders or alarms*: "Am I doing what I am supposed to be doing?"

Review: Strategies for Developing Adaptive Thinking

- *Use of thought records* to identify and label automatic thoughts.

Review the thought records you completed at home. If you were not able to complete any thought records, try to identify the obstacles that may have interfered, and use the problem-solving skills to determine the best way to work on automatic thinking. Did you have difficulty making time for home practice? Were the directions confusing? Was it difficult to see your thoughts in writing?

If you didn't do any thought records at home, it may be useful to practice doing one together with your therapist before moving on.

If you did complete a thought record during the week, then you should review each situation: the automatic thoughts and the thinking traps that you fell into. Do you see any patterns?

Sometimes it can be tricky to sort out thoughts from feelings. Your therapist can help with this, and you can practice asking yourself, "Is this what I was *thinking* or *feeling*?"

Skill: Formulating an Alternate Response

In this session, you will learn strategies to identify your thinking traps and develop more helpful thoughts. Our goal is to help you transform the unhelpful, interfering thoughts into more supportive, helpful coaching thoughts. In order to understand how powerful your thoughts can be, we like to tell a coaching story.

Coaching Story

This is a story about Little League Baseball. I talk about Little League Baseball because of the amazing parents and coaches involved. And by "amazing" I don't mean good. I mean extreme. You will see how it relates to ADHD and how you talk to yourself.

But this story doesn't start with the coaches or the parents: it starts with Johnny, who is a little league player in the outfield. His job is to catch fly balls and return them to the infield players. On this particular day, Johnny is in the outfield. And "crack!"—one of the players on the other team hits a fly ball. The ball is coming to Johnny. Johnny raises his glove. The ball is coming to him, it is coming to him. . . . Johnny jumps up as high as he can, but he is in the wrong place at the wrong time using the wrong strategy, so it goes over his head. Johnny misses the ball, and the other team scores a run.

Now there are a number of ways a coach can respond to this situation. Let's take the head coach who is named Coach A first. Coach A is the type of coach who will come out on the field and shout "I can't believe you missed that ball! Anyone could have caught it! My dog could have caught it! You screw up like that again and you'll be sitting on the bench! That was lousy!"

Coach A then storms off the field. At this point, if Johnny is anything like I am, he is standing there, tense, tight, trying not to cry, and praying that another ball is not hit to him. If a ball does come to him, Johnny will probably miss it. After all, he is tense, tight, and

---

may see four balls coming to him because of the tears in his eyes. Also, if we are Johnny's parents, we may see more profound changes after the game: Johnny, who typically places his baseball glove on the mantle, now throws it under his bed. And before the next game, he may complain that his stomach hurts, and say that perhaps he should not go to the game. This is the scenario with Coach A.

Now let's go back to the original event and play it differently. Johnny has just missed the fly ball, and now the assistant coach who is named Coach B comes out on the field. Coach B says "Well you missed that one. Here is what I want you to remember: fly balls always look like they are farther away than they really are. Also, it is much easier to run forward than to back-up. Because of this, I want you to prepare for the ball by taking a few extra steps backward. Run forward if you need to, but try to catch it at chest level so you can adjust your hand if you misjudge the ball. Let's see how you do next time."

Coach B leaves the field. How does Johnny feel? Well, he is not happy. After all, he missed the ball—but there are a number of important differences from the way he would feel with Coach A. He is not as tense or tight, and if a fly ball does come to him, he knows what to do differently to catch it. And because he does not have tears in his eyes, he may actually see the ball accurately. He may catch the next one.

So, if we were the type of parent who eventually wants Johnny to make the major leagues, we would pick Coach B because he teaches Johnny how to be a more effective player. Johnny knows what to do differently, may catch more balls, and may excel at the game. But if we don't care whether Johnny makes the major leagues—because baseball is a game, and one is supposed to be able to enjoy a game— then we would still pick Coach B. We pick Coach B because we care whether Johnny enjoys the game. With Coach B, Johnny knows what to do differently; he is not tight, tense, and ready to cry; he may catch a few balls; and he may enjoy the game. And he may continue to place his glove on the mantel.

Now, while we may all select Coach B for Johnny, we rarely choose the idea of Coach B for the way we talk to ourselves. Think about your last mistake. Did you say, "I can't believe I did that! I am so stupid! What a jerk!" These are Coach A thoughts, and they have approximately the same effect on us as they do on Johnny. They make us feel tense and tight, and they sometimes make us feel like crying.

And this style of coaching rarely makes us do better in the future. Even if you are only concerned about productivity (making the major league), you would still pick Coach B. And if you were concerned with enjoying life while guiding yourself effectively for both joy and productivity, you would still pick Coach B.

Keep in mind that we are not talking about how we coach ourselves in a baseball game. We are talking about how we coach ourselves in life and our enjoyment of life. People with excessive distress, and many with ADHD are often anxious and distressed, tend to talk to themselves this way.

During the next week, I would like you to listen to how you are coaching yourself. And if you hear Coach A, remember this story and see if you can replace Coach A with Coach B.

This story is meant to help you recognize negative, unhelpful thoughts as they pop up (Coach A thoughts) and to learn to develop more supportive, rational thinking (Coach B thoughts).

Let's go back to one of the thought records you previously completed. Review the automatic thoughts and thinking traps that you identified. If you have not completed a thought record yet, begin one now. The next step is to evaluate the helpfulness of each thought. The following questions are suggested prompts to help you objectively evaluate these thoughts:

- *What is the evidence that this thought is true?*
- *Is there an alternate explanation?*
- *What is the worst thing that can happen?*
- *Has this situation unreasonably grown in importance?*
- *What would a good coach say about this situation?*
- *Have I done what I can to control this situation?*
- *If I were to do anything else, would this help or hinder the situation?*
- *Am I worrying excessively about this?*
- *What would a good friend say to me about this situation?*
- *What would I say to a good friend about this situation if they were going through it?*
- *Why is this statement a thinking error?*
- *Is it helpful to focus on this thought at this moment?*

We now need to move to Worksheet 9: Five-Column Thought Record (located in the Appendix), which is the final version of the thought record that we will be using in this program. In the last—and very important—column, you formulate an alternative thought. The alternative thought is a statement that you can say to yourself to try to feel better about the situation. Keep in mind that we are not asking you to overlook all negative aspects of your thoughts. The idea is to come up with a more balanced, objective, and helpful way of thinking about the situation.

It is important to remember that sometimes thoughts can be true (for example, "I didn't study as much as I would have liked for that test"), and it is still not helpful to focus on them in a particular situation (for example, as you are walking into the classroom to take the test in question). In that case, the strategy is not necessarily to argue with yourself about whether or not the thought is true, but simply to point out that it is unhelpful to focus on the thought at this time.

For example, consider Johnny's thoughts from the coaching story: "I am so stupid. I missed that ball. I'll never become a good baseball player. I'll always be a failure." The goal would be for him to acknowledge that he missed the ball on this one occasion but that he has caught others in the past (no magnification/minimization), to recognize that there are additional skills he can learn to help him become a better player (no fortune telling), and to see himself as having as good a chance as the next boy to become a good ball player (no catastrophizing). Figure 9.1 shows some examples of negative/unhelpful thoughts and the corresponding more balanced, helpful alternate responses.

Potential Pitfalls

We have discussed several different types of thinking traps that can contribute to negative feelings and behaviors. While it is important to be familiar with the types of traps you may be falling into, don't get stuck trying to find the exact type of trap that corresponds with your thought. Your thought may fit into more than one category, and often these categories of thinking traps overlap. Your goal is to recognize that your automatic thought might be a thinking trap, to understand why this is true, and, most importantly, to come up with an alternative response.

Time and Situation	Automatic Thoughts (Coach A)	Mood and Intensity	Thinking Trap	Alternative Thought (Coach B)
Writing an English paper.	I have to write the entire paper today	Overwhelmed (80)	All or nothing thinking	I don't need to do it all today. I can start today and finish it up tomorrow.
	I must do this perfectly.	Anxious (75)	All or nothing thinking	Even if it isn't perfect, it makes sense to start on a draft.
	If I do not finish, my teacher will be upset.	Depressed (60)	Jumping to conclusions (mind reading)	My teacher has been really understanding in the past, so I don't think she will react any differently now.
	If the paper is not perfect, I will fail out of school and I won't be able to get into college.	Anxious (95)	Jumping to conclusions (fortune telling), Catastrophizing	Even if I don't get a good grade on this paper, it is unlikely that I will fail out of school. I have a lot of other grades that are good.
	Actually, I don't need to start the paper today because I can do it on Sunday night.	Relieved (100)	Overly optimistic thinking	I know from past experience that papers take longer than I think. I'll be really stressed on Sunday night if I don't start it before then.

Figure 9.1

Sample completed five-column thought record.

Developing an alternative response to your negative thoughts may be tricky at first. Refer to the suggested questions listed earlier (for example, *What would you say to a good friend about this situation if they were going through it?*). Also, keep in mind that your thoughts and feelings about the situation may not completely change immediately after you come up with the alternative response. However, if you repeat the more helpful responses to yourself, they will begin to replace the negative, automatic thoughts you initially had.

Instructions for Completing a Five-Column Thought Record

The purpose of doing this exercise is to help you cope better when you are feeling stressed. Throughout the week, when you are feeling stressed, sad, or overwhelmed, list your thoughts for each situation on Worksheet 9. If you are anticipating a stressful situation or a task that is making you feel overwhelmed, write out your thoughts about this situation. If a situation has already passed, and you find that you are thinking about it negatively, list your thoughts for this situation.

- The *first column* is for you to write a description of the situation.
- The *second column* is for you to list your thoughts during a stressful, overwhelming, or uncontrollable situation.
- The *third column* is for you to write down what emotions you are having and what your mood is like when thinking these thoughts (for example, depressed, sad, angry).
- The *fourth column* is for you to see if your thoughts match the list of "thinking traps" These may include
  - *All or nothing thinking*
  - *Overgeneralization*
  - *Mental filter*
  - *Disqualifying the positive*
  - *Jumping to conclusions*
    - *Mind reading*
    - *Fortune telling*
  - *Magnification/Minimization*
  - *Catastrophizing*
  - *Emotional reasoning*
  - *"Should" statements*
  - *Labeling and mislabeling*
  - *Personalization*
  - *Maladaptive thinking*
  - *Overly optimistic thinking*
- The *last column* is for you to try to come up with an alternative thought to replace each negative automatic thought—or the most important negative automatic thought. The *alternative thought* is a statement that you can say to yourself to try to feel better about the situation. Questions to help come up with this alternative thought can include
  - *What is the evidence that this thought is true?*
  - *Is there an alternate explanation?*
  - *What is the worst thing that can happen?*
  - *Has this situation unreasonably grown in importance?*
  - *What would a good coach say about this situation?*
  - *Have I done what I can do to control it?*
  - *If I were to do anything else, would this help or hinder the situation?*
  - *Am I worrying excessively about this?*

- *What would a good friend say to me about this situation?*
- *What would I say to a good friend about this situation if they were going through it?*
- *Why is this statement a thinking error?*
- *Is it helpful to focus on this thought at this moment?*

Practice

As you are learning in this treatment, practicing new skills is vital so that you become familiar with them, are able to easily use the tools, and begin to see the positive results that can emerge when you consistently use these CBT strategies. Recognize that, at first, when you are learning a new skill, it may feel awkward, may be confusing, and may require effort to implement. That's ok! The more you practice, the easier it will become.

- Continue to use the calendar every day to keep track of your schedule and put new tasks on the task list every day.
- Use and look at the task list and calendar *every day*!
- Use your priority ratings.
- Practice doing your tasks according to the priority ratings.
- Carry over tasks that are not completed to the next day's task list.
- Practice using Worksheet 3: Problem-Solving: Selection of Action Plan or Worksheet 4: Problem-Solving: Pick Three for at least one item on the task list.
- Practice breaking down one large task from the task list into smaller steps.
- Use the organizational systems developed in this program.
- Use the distractibility delay when working on boring or unattractive tasks.
- Use your skills to reduce distraction in your homework environment.
- Start putting important items in specific places.
- Use reminders to check in with yourself to see if you have become distracted when you are trying to focus on completing a task.
- Read the "Instructions for Completing a Five-Column Thought Record" earlier in this chapter.
- Write out examples of thoughts on Worksheet 9 for at least two situations during the week.

CHAPTER 10

Session 10: How Can Parents Help? Second Parent/Adolescent Session

OVERVIEW

The main goal of this chapter is for you and your parents to check in with your therapist and discuss how the treatment program is going so far. Your therapist will revisit the goals that you and your parents set at the beginning of the treatment program, talk about how well everything is going with your parents' level of involvement in the treatment, and discuss how things are going with the reward system that you and your parents set up in the earlier parent/adolescent session.

Your therapist will also talk about the changes you have made so far as the result of this treatment program and will help you and your parents set reasonable expectations for delayed improvements and for continuing to use the skills after this treatment program has ended. Your therapist will discuss whether you would like to complete the optional session on procrastination (most people choose to do this) and will talk about home practice activities.

GOALS

- Continue to monitor your progress
- Review your continual use of skills from previous chapters
- Review thought records completed at home

- Review parent involvement in treatment and troubleshoot any issues or problems
- Review use of the reward system
- Review changes that you and your family have made as a result of your participation in this treatment program
- Review expectations and discuss the potential for delayed improvement
- Identify additional situations that might require adaptive thinking for home practice
- Evaluate your need to complete the optional session on procrastination
- Agree on home practice activities and anticipate difficulties using these techniques

Review of Symptom Checklist

As you have been doing each week, complete the attention-deficit/hyperactivity disorder (ADHD) symptom checklist that you and your therapist are using to track your symptoms. Be sure to review your score and take note of symptoms that have improved and those that are still problematic and share this information with your therapist.

Score: _____   **Date:** _____

Review of Medication Adherence

Using the ADHD Medication Form, record your prescribed dosage of medication and indicate the number of doses you actually took. Think about reasons for missed doses such as being distracted, running out of medication, your parents forgetting to give you your medication, or your thoughts about not wanting/needing to take medication. You should repeat this exercise at the beginning of every therapy session and share it with your therapist so that it can be discussed in therapy.

ADHD Medication Form

How many times were you supposed to take your ADHD medicine this week? _____

How many times did you actually take your ADHD medicine this week? _____

Reasons for missed doses: _____

_____

_____

Review of Previous Chapters

Each week you should review your progress implementing skills from each of the previous chapters. It is important to acknowledge the successes you have achieved and to problem-solve around any difficulties.

Review: Tools for Organization and Planning

- *Use of calendar for managing your schedule*: At this point, you should discuss any problems that you are having with using your calendar system.
- *Use of task list system*: Review any difficulties that you are having with using your task list on a daily basis.
- *Use of priority ratings*: If you are having any trouble with prioritizing tasks, this should be discussed at this point.
- *Use of problem-solving (selecting an action plan) and breaking down large tasks into small steps*: Consider your use of these strategies and practice one or both skills using examples from your current task list.

Review: Tools for Reducing Distractibility

- *Use of the strategy of breaking down tasks into manageable chunks*: At this point, you should discuss with your therapist any problems that you are having with breaking down tasks.
- *Use of the distractibility delay*: Review any difficulties that you are having with the distractibility delay technique.
- *Use of strategy to remove distractions from the environment.*
- *Use of strategy to have a specific place* for each important object.
- *Use of reminders or alarms*: "Am I doing what I am supposed to be doing?"

Review: Strategies for Developing Adaptive Thinking

- *Use of thought records* to identify and label automatic thoughts.
- *Use of thought records* to identify alternative thoughts.

Review: Parent Involvement in Treatment

You and your parents should discuss how things are going with the treatment program, especially those aspects that involve your parents. You can talk about the things that are going well and also about things that are not going so well so that your therapist can help you figure out a way to improve the situation. For example, if you had agreed that your parent(s) would remind you to check your homework and set priorities each evening, but this has been turning into a big argument and doesn't feel very helpful, you could bring this up and try to work with your therapist to find a solution that will work better for everyone.

Review: Reward System

You and your parents should talk about how well the reward system that you developed at the earlier parent/adolescent session is working. If big issues have come up, you have probably already discussed them. However, this is a good opportunity to really do a comprehensive review of the system. Again, you can talk about what is working well and also the things that aren't working well. For example, if you agreed on a particular reward but are finding that it just isn't that motivating for you, you might think about whether a different reward might be better. Also, if you are finding that you are getting annoyed because you need to remind your parents to give you the rewards, that would be a good thing to discuss as well.

Your therapist will talk with you and your parents about how to continue to check in and adjust the reward system after treatment ends. Also, there may be a time in the future (such as when you leave for college) when you might want to make a reward system for yourself that doesn't involve your parents (like allowing yourself to do something special or relaxing after you have competed certain tasks).

Review: Behavioral Changes That You and Your Parents Have Made as a Result of Participation in This Program

Your therapist will review all changes/improvements that you and your parent(s) have made as a result of participating in this treatment. This program is hard work, and it is really important for all of you to give yourselves credit for everything you have done so far. It is really difficult to change behaviors, and you will continue to see the benefits of the positive changes you have made for many years to come.

Review: Expectations and Potential for Delayed Improvements

At this point, you and your parents should review the list of initial goals for treatment (Worksheet 1: Goals of CBT) that you and your parents created. Look at how close you are to reaching the goals set out at the beginning of treatment. Talk with your therapist about how realistic these goals were and also discuss the possibility for continued progress toward the goals if you maintain the skills learned in the treatment. Sometimes change can take a long time, and you may not see the impact for a while. For example, if one of your goals was to have better grades, it may take a while to see the impact as you are learning to prioritize homework, plan ahead for larger projects or papers, and so on. Also, your grades are an average across the term, semester, or year, so the portions of that time period when you weren't using this program will be averaged in. It is important to give yourself credit for being willing to engage in this program and know that these small changes will continue to help you improve in the future.

Planning for Future Treatment

Congratulations!! You have now completed the core elements of cognitive behavior therapy (CBT) for ADHD. Again, review Worksheet 1 to determine whether to begin the optional session on how to handle procrastination, to do more review work on sessions that were already completed, or to continue to the final session of treatment, which focuses on how to keep going with the skills after treatment has ended.

Potential Pitfalls

You have done a lot of work to get to this point! You may feel like taking a break or believe that you have done enough work and will no longer have any difficulties related to ADHD. The most important message to emphasize here is that you need to PRACTICE, PRACTICE, PRACTICE!!! This will ensure that newly learned skills become permanent and that your efforts will continue to pay off.

Practice

As you are learning in this treatment, practicing new skills is vital so that you become familiar with them, are able to easily use the tools, and begin to see the positive results that can emerge when you consistently use these CBT strategies. Recognize that, at first, when you are learning a new skill, it may feel awkward, may be confusing, and may require effort to implement. That's ok! The more you practice, the easier it will become.

- Continue practicing skills learned in previous sessions.
- Continue to use cognitive techniques for situations involving stress.
- Remember to consider any anticipated problems completing the home practice.
- Implement any changes that you and your parents agreed upon to your reward system and other systems.

Additional Skills

CHAPTER 11

Session 11: Don't Put It Off—Stop Procrastinating

This session will be helpful if you have been having significant difficulties with procrastination. For individuals with attention-deficit/hyperactivity disorder (ADHD), procrastination can be a result of what we call *cognitive avoidance*—the deliberate postponing of tasks because you can focus more easily when you are closer to the deadline. Procrastinating may also result from *perfectionism* (thinking something needs to be perfect, which is not a realistic goal).

This chapter on procrastination is a single session because it uses several of the skills you have already learned in previous sessions, including (1) reframing thoughts such as "This paper needs to be perfect or I can't turn it in" (refer back to Chapter 9); (2) breaking down tasks into manageable steps (refer back to Chapter 4); and (3) learning to set realistic goals for completing individual steps rather than the entire task (refer back to Chapter 4).

Learning skills for managing procrastination will help you to:

- Understand why procrastination sometimes seems like a great idea
- Anticipate the problems caused by procrastination
- Use skills for problem-solving around procrastination
- Use adaptive thinking skills for managing procrastination

- Continue to monitor your progress
- Review your continual use of skills from previous chapters
- Learn why procrastination is so appealing and why it causes so many problems
- Use Worksheet 10: Pros and Cons of Procrastination (located in the Appendix) to help you decide whether or not to procrastinate
- Adapt problem-solving to the issue of procrastination
- Use adaptive thinking for managing procrastination
- Agree on home practice activities and anticipate difficulties using these techniques

Review of Symptom Checklist

As you have been doing each week, complete the ADHD symptom checklist that you and your therapist are using to track your symptoms. Be sure to review your score and take note of symptoms that have improved and those that are still problematic and share this information with your therapist.

Score: _____   **Date:** _____

Review of Medication Adherence

Using the ADHD Medication Form, record your prescribed dosage of medication and indicate the number of doses you actually took. Think about reasons for missed doses such as being distracted, running out of medication, your parents forgetting to give you your medication, or your thoughts about not wanting/needing to take medication. You should repeat this exercise at the beginning of every therapy session and share it with your therapist so that it can be discussed in therapy.

ADHD Medication Form

How many times were you supposed to take your ADHD medicine this week? _____

How many times did you actually take your ADHD medicine this week? _____

Reasons for missed doses: _____

_____

_____

Review of Previous Chapters

Each week you should review your progress implementing skills from each of the previous chapters. It is important to acknowledge the successes you have achieved and to problem-solve around any difficulties.

Review: Tools for Organization and Planning

- *Use of calendar for managing your schedule*: At this point, you should discuss any problems that you are having with using your calendar system.
- *Use of task list system*: Review any difficulties that you are having with using your task list on a daily basis.
- *Use of priority ratings*: If you are having any trouble with prioritizing tasks, this should be discussed at this point.
- *Use of problem-solving (selecting an action plan) and breaking down large tasks into small steps*: Consider your use of these strategies and practice one or both skills using examples from your current task list.

Review: Tools for Reducing Distractibility

- *Use of the strategy of breaking down tasks into manageable chunks*: At this point, you should discuss with your therapist any problems that you are having with breaking down tasks.
- *Use of the distractibility delay*: Review any difficulties that you are having with the distractibility delay technique.
- *Use of strategy to remove distractions from the environment.*
- *Use of strategy to have a specific place* for each important object.
- *Use of reminders or alarms*: "Am I doing what I am supposed to be doing?"

Review: Strategies for Developing Adaptive Thinking

- *Use of thought records* to identify and label automatic thoughts.
- *Use of thought records* to identify alternative thoughts.

Introduction to Procrastination

Many people with ADHD struggle with procrastination. In this chapter, you will review your history with procrastination and try to identify the areas in which it has caused problems for you. You will also learn to think about the reasons behind your procrastination. Once you figure out why you tend to procrastinate, you will be able to use skills to decrease the interference of procrastination.

The Attractiveness of Procrastination

While procrastination can cause anxiety and anguish, there are also reasons why it *seems* desirable or easier to postpone tasks. Some reasons are:

- Perfectionism/fear of negative evaluation for a less than perfect product.
- The idea that it is difficult to get started unless the time pressure is there.
- The issue seems overwhelming.
- You have difficulty finding a starting point.
- The tasks in question are not attractive.
- You want to wait until you have enough time (this usually never comes).

Do any of these reasons sound familiar to you? Think about the reasons that seem to cause you to procrastinate. Can you think of any reasons that are not listed here?

The Consequences of Procrastination

As we discussed, procrastination can appear to be a good option if it helps you avoid a negative feeling or if you *think* that the time/environment must be just right before you can begin a task. Unfortunately, these potential benefits are often outweighed by far more negative consequences of procrastination, including:

- It is stressful waiting until the last minute to complete a task.
- The task, which is unattractive in the first place, is even worse when you need to drop all of your other activities and focus 100% of your time and attention on that task (for example, putting off writing a paper and then needing to pull an all-nighter to get it done).
- There may be times when you miss the deadline and there is a penalty (for example, you get a lower grade on a paper, you miss the deadline to apply to a school or a program).
- You feel worse about yourself later.
- The final product is not as good as it could have been.
- Ignoring the problem usually makes it worse and even harder to solve later.

Do you recognize any of these consequences? Have you experienced them? Think about how procrastination has had negative consequences for you. Can you think of any negative consequences that are not listed here?

Skill: Evaluating the Pros and Cons of Procrastination

Sometimes it can be useful to evaluate pros and cons of an action before making a decision. In this way, "deciding to procrastinate" on a task can be seen as a decision that you might be making. Accordingly, you can use Worksheet 10: Pros and Cons of Procrastination, located in the Appendix, to help you make a decision about what to do.

Remember that sometimes the short-term pros and cons are different from the long-term pros and cons, so be sure to evaluate both.

Worksheet 10 will assist you in objectively rating the pros and cons of procrastination. To get started, think about a situation where you might be tempted to procrastinate. Then fill in the boxes on the worksheet, first writing out the short-term pros and cons and then writing out the long-term pros and cons. Often, when people look at this completed worksheet, they observe that, in the short term, the pros may outweigh the cons but, in the long term, there are more cons.

Unfortunately, it is sometimes difficult to remember the pros and cons in the moment when you are facing an overwhelming task. Taking a time out to review the pros and the cons can be useful at these times.

Skill: Adapting Problem-Solving to the Issue of Procrastination

In Chapter 4 of this workbook, you learned to use skills for problem-solving. When a task feels overwhelming or you are uncertain about where to begin, you are more likely to procrastinate. Breaking down the task into small steps will help avoid this. Remember that each step should feel completely doable. If it doesn't, break down the step even further. Alternatively, rather than attempting to work on the whole problem, you may want to target only one or two smaller goals. You can refer to Worksheets 3, 4, and 5 to help with problem-solving.

Another trap that individuals can fall into is setting unreasonable goals. Recall that each step should be realistic. The skills you learned for managing distractibility (refer to Chapters 6 and 7) will also be useful here. If you know that you are generally able to work on unpleasant tasks for 15 minutes, then you should try to break down each step into goals that can be completed in this timeframe.

Skill: Using Adaptive Thinking to Help with Procrastination

As you have learned, your thoughts can play a powerful role in shaping how you feel about a situation, and they can influence your actions in a situation. Negative and/or unhelpful automatic thoughts can also greatly contribute to procrastination. Using thought records will help you create balanced, helpful thoughts that will decrease procrastination.

Remember, there are five steps involved in completing the thought record. You can do this on the form provided (Worksheet 9: Five-Column Thought Record, located in the Appendix) or electronically.

1. List the situation contributing to procrastination.
2. List the automatic thoughts regarding the task or goal (Coach A thoughts).
3. List your mood and the intensity of your mood.
4. Refer to the list of thinking traps to evaluate your thoughts.
5. Formulate alternative thoughts to the original thoughts (Coach B thoughts).

Example

As you know, you need to practice new skills so that they will come easily to you when you need them.

- Think about a specific task or issue about which you have been procrastinating.
- Specifically try to use each of the above skills for this task or issue.
- Use problem-solving to help break down the task into manageable steps.
- Write down the steps on your master task list.
- Next, use Worksheet 9: Five-Column Thought Record, to list the automatic thoughts you are having about getting started.
- Finally, on Worksheet 9, identify the appropriate thinking traps and try to come up with alternative thoughts.

Potential Pitfalls

Although you may have struggled with procrastination for many years, it is important to remember that you *can* use the strategies you have already learned to decrease the interference of procrastination. If you are unsure about whether these strategies will help, do an experiment. For 1 month, commit to using these skills each day and see how well you do. Chances are you are going to see the results quickly, and it will then be easier to practice your newly learned skills.

- Plan a reasonable goal or two to start, from the list of steps that you have outlined on your master task list.
- Think of a way that you can reward yourself upon completion of the goals. You might want to set up rewards for intermediate steps toward your goals to help keep you motivated (for example, give yourself a small reward for each paragraph or page that you write and a larger reward when the paper is done).
- Review your use of skills from the previous sessions of treatment. Be sure to write down any questions or difficulties you may be having so that you can discuss them with your therapist at the final session.

CHAPTER 12 ▶ Session 12: Keeping It Going

Thinking About the End of Treatment

Congratulations! You are now reaching the end of a dozen chapters' worth of information and skills designed to help you treat the distress and impairment of your attention-deficit/hyperactivity disorder (ADHD). However, the completion of this workbook and the end of your sessions with your therapist do not equal the end of your program of treatment.

The strategies and skills that you learned as part of this program now need to be practiced regularly so that they become more automatic. In other words, the end of regular sessions with your therapist is the starting point of your own program of treatment, where you work to lock in and extend the skills and strategies that you have learned. If you practice these skills on a daily or weekly basis, you will help ensure that you continue to maintain or extend the benefits you have achieved.

To begin your transition to this next phase of treatment—where you take over the role of the therapist in directing your own treatment—it is important for you to recognize all that you have achieved so far.

Goals

- Continue to monitor your progress
- Review home practice of skills that you have already learned
- Review your progress in therapy
- Review the strategies you have learned in this treatment and discuss which strategies were the most valuable for you

- Discuss how to maintain the gains you have made
- Learn how to troubleshoot if you encounter difficulties with your ADHD symptoms in the future

Review of Symptom Checklist

As you have been doing each week, complete the ADHD symptom checklist that you and your therapist are using to track your symptoms. Be sure to review your score and take note of symptoms that have improved and those that are still problematic and share this information with your therapist.

Score: _____   **Date:** _____

Please take several moments with your therapist to review your symptom scores that you wrote in at the beginning of each chapter. Using Figure 12.1, you may want to re-copy the scores here so that you can see when

Chapter	Score
1	
2	
3	
4	
5	
6	
7	
8	
9	
10	
11	
12	
Other	

Figure 12.1

Symptom checklist scores.

and where during the course of treatment you made particular gains. Remember, the benefits from any particular treatment strategy may not appear until it has been practiced for several weeks.

Review of Medication Adherence

Using the ADHD Medication Form, record your prescribed dosage of medication and indicate the number of doses you actually took. Think about reasons for missed doses such as being distracted, running out of medication, your parents forgetting to give you your medication, or your thoughts about not wanting/needing to take medication. You should repeat this exercise at the beginning of every therapy session and share it with your therapist so that it can be discussed in therapy.

ADHD Medication Form

How many times were you supposed to take your ADHD medicine this week? _____

How many times did you actually take your ADHD medicine this week? _____

Reasons for missed doses: _____

_____

_____

Examining What Was Valuable for You

Consider what strategies might have been the most useful for you during the program. Worksheet 11: Treatment Strategies and Usefulness, found in the Appendix, summarizes many of the strategies you have tried. Using this worksheet, please rate the usefulness of each strategy to you (0, "Didn't help at all" to 100, "Was extremely important for me"). Take some time to provide notes to yourself about why you think each strategy worked or didn't work to help you decide which strategies might be most helpful for you to continue to practice over the next month.

Successful treatment does not mean that you will not have future difficulties with ADHD symptoms. For most problems, symptoms can wax and wane over time. The key to maintaining treatment gains in the long run is to be prepared for the periods of increased difficulties.

These periods are not signs that the treatment failed you or that you failed the treatment. Instead, these periods are signals that you need to apply the skills that you learned in treatment. To help you refresh your skills, please look at Figure 12.2. The purpose of this chart is to remind you of the importance of practicing skills and to help you think through which strategies might be important for you to continue practicing.

As you end treatment, schedule review sessions with yourself. You might do this on the day and time when you have been meeting with your

Symptoms	Skills to Consider	Chapter(s) to Review
Failing to give adequate attention to details / making careless mistakes in work or other activities	Recheck your attention span and your ability to break down activities into units where you can sustain attention. Use your cues (alarm) to remind you of core responsibilities at hand.	4, 6, 7
Difficulty sustaining attention in tasks	Check your management of your space. (Are your environments too distracting?)	7
Difficulty organizing tasks in terms of importance	Use your prioritization system. Use your triage and organizational systems.	1, 3, 4, 5
Procrastination	Use problem-solving and adaptive thinking. Break down large tasks into smaller steps.	4, 8, 9, 11
Losing things necessary for tasks or activities	Use a single work area. Use your triage and organizational systems. Work with another person to reduce clutter.	1, 3, 5, 7
Easily distracted by things going on in the environment	Manage your environment, and use your distractibility delay.	6, 7
Forgetful in daily activities	Use your alarm system and your task list along with your calendar.	1, 3, 7
Negative/Unhelpful thoughts	Use self-coaching skills	8, 9

Figure 12.2

Trouble-shooting difficulties chart.

therapist. The first step in being prepared for this upcoming review is to schedule it. Since you are now at the end of this program, you know exactly where you keep your calendar—it is in the location that you identified (and if it isn't there, this might be a first reminder to work harder to always return your important tools to your selected spot). Please schedule a review session with yourself for 1 month from now. Use Worksheet 12: 1 Month Review, located in the Appendix, for this self-review.

Troubleshooting Your Difficulties

If you find that some of your symptoms are causing trouble for you in the future, it may be helpful to match the symptoms you are experiencing with some of the specific strategies used in this treatment. Look at Figure 12.2 and see if it helps you identify some of the strategies that may be helpful to practice.

Finally, you may want to use the problem-solving worksheet in Chapter 4 (Worksheets 3 and 4, located in the Appendix) to more carefully consider any difficulties with symptoms you are currently having. And if these strategies do not help, consider getting additional input from family or friends or schedule a booster session with your therapist.

We wish you the best in continuing to use these skills!

Some of the worksheets in this Appendix need to be completed multiple times throughout this treatment program. Either your therapist will provide copies for you, or you can download blank copies from the TreatmentsThatWork™ website at www.oup.com/adolescentADHD.

Worksheet 1

Goals of Cognitive Behavioral Therapy (CBT)

Goal of CBT	Controllability (as a percent)	Short or long term

Worksheet 2

Task List

Priority rating	Task	Date put on list	Date completed
A			
A			
.			
.			
B			
.			
.			
.			
.			
.			
.			
C			
.			
.			
.			
.			
.			
.			

Note: This format can be used for a paper system. Many electronic systems allow for making priority ratings as well. You should use the system that best fits your needs.

Worksheet 3

Problem-Solving: Selection of Action Plan

Statement of the problem: __READING COMPREHENSION ON SCHOOL WORK__

Instructions for chart:

1. List all of the possible solutions that you can think of. List them even if you think they don't make sense or you don't think you would do them. The point is to come up with *as many solutions as possible*.

2. List the pros and cons of each solution.

3. After listing the pros and cons of each, review the whole list, and give a rating to each solution.

4. Use additional copies of this sheet as needed (even if it's for the same problem).

Possible solution	Pros of solution	Cons of solution	Overall rating of solution (1–10)
READING MORE OFTEN			5
READ SLOWER TO NOT MAKE MISTAKES	MORE AWARE MAKING USE OF ACCOMODATIONS	TAKES LONGER NOT 100% EFFECTIVE	1
WEARING GLASSES TO HELP READ			4
ASK FOR ACCOMODATIONS –TIME, BIG TEXT			3
HIGHLIGHT, BOLD TEXT, UNDERLINE	HELPS W/ VISUAL LEARNING SIMPLIFY	NOT ALWAYS AVAILABLE CAN GET MESSY	2

Worksheet 4

Problem-Solving: Pick Three

Description of problem:_____

Possible solution	Pros of solution	Cons of solution	Rating

"Winning" solution_____

Worksheet 5

Problem-Solving: Small Steps

Description of large task:_____

What is the first small step?	
What is the second small step?	
What is the third small step?	
What is the fourth small step?	

Worksheet 6

Strategies for Reducing Distractions

Distraction	Distraction reduction strategy

Three-Column Thought Record

Time and situation	Automatic thoughts	Mood and intensity

Worksheet 8

Four-Column Thought Record

Time and situation	Automatic thoughts	Mood and intensity	Thinking trap

Five-Column Thought Record

Time and situation	Automatic thought (Coach A)	Mood and intensity	Thinking trap	Alternative thought (Coach B)
	SHE'S MAD AT ME → I DID SOMETHING WRONG	WORRIED → 6/10	FORTUNE TELLING/ PERSONALIZA -TION →	SHE MIGHT HAVE SOMETHING GOING ON AT HOME.

Worksheet 10

Pros and Cons of Procrastination

	Short term	Long term
Pros	GETTING TO DO A FUN ACTIVITY: -KNITTING/CRAFTS -HANG W/ FRIEND -SLEEPING MORE MOTIVATION TO COMPLETE ASSIGNMENT	-BETTER MENTAL HEALTH
Cons	-STILL HAVE TO COMPLETE ASSIGNMENT -MORE STRESS -STILL IN THE BACK OF MY MIND -DECREASED SELF-CONFIDENCE	-MORE STRESS -RUSHED, DECREASE OF PERFORMANCE/GRADES -MAKES PROBLEM MORE DIFFICULT -DEADLINE IS NOT MET, MISSING WORK

Worksheet 11

Treatment Strategies and Usefulness

Please rate the usefulness of each strategy to you (0 "Didn't help at all" to 100 "Was extremely important for me"). Also, take some time to provide notes to yourself about why you think each strategy worked or didn't work for you, and decide which strategies might be most helpful for you to practice over the next month.

Treatment strategies	Usefulness ratings	Notes about your application/usefulness of the strategy
Review: Tools for Organization and Planning: ▪ Calendar for managing your schedule ▪ Task list system ▪ Priority ratings ▪ Problem-solving (selecting an action plan) ▪ Breaking down large tasks into small steps ▪ Rewards to increase motivation to complete tasks ▪ Organizational systems Review: Strategies for Managing Distractibility: ▪ Breaking tasks down into manageable chunks and use of breaks in between tasks ▪ Distractibility delay ▪ Removing distractions from the environment ▪ Having specific places for important objects ▪ Reminders/Alarms—"Am I doing what I'm supposed to be doing?" Review: Adaptive Thinking: ▪ Writing down negative/unhelpful thoughts ▪ Reviewing list of thinking traps ▪ Using Coach B thinking to create balanced, helpful thoughts		

Worksheet 12

One-Month Review

Date of review: _____

---

1. What skills have you been practicing well?

2. Where do you still have troubles?

3. Can you place the troubles in one of the specific areas used in this treatment?

4. Have you reviewed the skills most relevant to your difficulties? (Which skills are these?)

5. Have you reviewed Worksheet 11: Treatment Strategies and Usefulness, where you wrote those skills that were most helpful to you in the first phase of this treatment? Do you need to reapply these skills or strategies?

Bibliography

American Psychiatric Association. (2013). *Diagnostic and statistical manual of mental disorders* (5th ed.). Washington, DC: American Psychiatric Association.

Barkley, R. A. (1998). *Attention-deficit hyperactivity disorder: A handbook for diagnosis and treatment* (2nd ed.). New York: Guilford Press.

Craske, M. H., & Barlow, D. H. (2006). *Mastery of your anxiety and worry: Client workbook* (2nd ed.). New York: Oxford.

D'Zurilla, T. J. (1986). *Problem-solving therapy: A social competence approach to clinical interventions.* New York: Springer.

Hallowell, E. M. (1995). Psychotherapy of adult attention deficit disorder. In K. G. Nadeau (Ed.), *A comprehensive guide to attention deficit disorder in adults: Research, diagnosis and treatment* (pp. 146–167). New York: Brunner/Mazel.

Hope, D. A., Heimberg, R. H., Juster, H. R., & Turk, C. L. (2000). *Managing social anxiety: A cognitive behavioral therapy approach.* Boulder, CO: Graywind Publications.

Kelly, K., & Ramundo, P. (2006). *You mean I'm not lazy, stupid or crazy?!* New York: Scribner.

Knouse, L. E., & Mitchell, J. T. (2015). Incautiously optimistic: Positively valenced cognitive avoidance in adults with ADHD. *Cognitive and Behavioral Practice, 22*(2), 192–202.

Mayes, V. (1998). *A clinician's handbook for attention-deficit hyperactivity disorder in adults.* Unpublished dissertation. Colorado State University.

McDermott, S. P. (2000). Cognitive therapy of adults with attention-deficit hyperactivity disorder. In T. Brown (Ed.), *Attention deficit disorders and comorbidity in children, adolescents and adults* (pp. 569–607). Washington, DC: American Psychiatric Press.

Nadeau, K. G. (1995). Life management skills for the adult with ADD. In K. G. Nadeau (Ed.), *A comprehensive guide to attention deficit disorder in adults: Research, diagnosis and treatment* (pp. 191–217). New York: Brunner/Mazel.

Nezu, A. M., Nezu, C. M., Friedman, S. H., Faddis, S., & Houts, P. S. (1998). *Helping cancer patients cope: A problem-solving approach.* Washington, DC: American Psychological Association.

Otto, M. (2000). Stories and metaphors in cognitive-behavior therapy. *Cognitive and Behavioral Practice, 69*, 166–172.

Otto, M. W., Jones, J. C., Craske, M. G., & Barlow, D. H. (1996). *Stopping anxiety medication: Panic control therapy for benzodiazepine discontinuation (therapist guide).* San Antonio, TX: Psychological Corporation.

Otto, M. W., & Pollack, M. H. (2009). *Stopping anxiety medication—Therapist guide* (2nd ed.). New York: Oxford.

Persons, J. B. (1989). *Cognitive therapy in practice: A case formulation approach.* New York: Norton.

Safren, S. A., Otto, M. W., Sprich, S., Perlman, C. L., Wilens, T. E., & Biederman, J. (2005). Cognitive behavioral therapy for ADHD in medication-treated adults with continued symptoms. *Behaviour Research and Therapy, 43*, 831–842.

Safren, S. A., Sprich, S., Chulvick, S., & Otto, M. W. (2004). Psychosocial treatments for adults with attention-deficit/hyperactivity disorder. *Psychiatric Clinics of North America, 27*(2), 349–360.

Safren, S. A., Sprich, S., Mimiaga, M. J., Surman, C., Knouse, L., Groves, M., & Otto, M. W. (2010). Cognitive behavioral therapy vs relaxation with educational support for medication-treated adults with ADHD and persistent symptoms: A randomized controlled trial. *JAMA, 304*(8), 875–880.

Sprich, S. E., Burbridge, J., Lerner, J. A., & Safren, S. A. (2015). Cognitive-behavioral therapy for ADHD in adolescents: Clinical considerations and a case series. *Cognitive and Behavioral Practice, 22*(2), 116–126.

Sprich, S. E., Safren, S. A., Finkelstein, D., Remmert, J. E., & Hammerness, P. (2016). A randomized controlled trial of cognitive behavioral therapy for ADHD in medication-treated adolescents, *Journal of Child Psychology and Psychiatry, 57*(11), 1218–1226.

Susan E. Sprich received her BA in Psychology from the University of Pennsylvania and her PhD in Clinical Psychology from The University at Albany, State University of New York. She completed her clinical psychology internship training and postdoctoral training at Massachusetts General Hospital/Harvard Medical School, and has been affiliated with Massachusetts General Hospital (MGH) since 1994. She has served as the Director of the Cognitive-Behavioral Therapy Program at MGH since 2014. She was appointed as the Director of Postgraduate Psychology Education for the MGH Psychiatry Academy in 2015. She is an Assistant Professor in Psychology at Harvard Medical School. Dr. Sprich is a co-author of 27 chapters and articles on a range of topics including psychosocial treatments for ADHD in adults and adolescents, trichotillomania, and social anxiety. She is the co-author of *Mastering Your Adult ADHD—Therapist Guide* and *Client Workbook*, published by Oxford University Press in the Treatments *ThatWork* series. She served as a co-editor of the *MGH CBT Handbook*, published by Springer. She teaches and supervises psychology interns and psychiatry residents at Massachusetts General Hospital. She is the Assistant Director of the Psychology Internship Program at MGH. She was the recipient of the Emerson Award from MGH for her dissertation research and was awarded a Scholars in Medicine Fellowship through Harvard Medical School. She was given an award for excellence in mentoring by the psychology interns in 2015 and the Behavioral Medicine Service award in 2018. Dr. Sprich has been involved in research projects focused on ADHD, BDD, OCD, and Autism Spectrum Disorders. Dr. Sprich has extensive clinical experience working with ADHD, anxiety, Trichotillomania, OCD, and other Obsessive-Compulsive Spectrum Disorders.

Steven A. Safren received his BA from Brandeis University and his PhD from The University at Albany, State University of New York. He completed his clinical psychology internship and postdoctoral fellowship at Harvard Medical School/Massachusetts General Hospital (MGH), where he worked until 2015. He is currently a Professor and Cooper Fellow in the Department of Psychology at the University of Miami. He is also the founding Director of the UM Center for HIV and Research in

Mental Health (NIMH-funded Developmental AIDS Research Center D-ARC) and the Health Promotion and Care research program (https://hpac.psy.miami.edu/). Before he moved to Miami, he served in various roles in the Harvard Medical School system and MGH: he was a Professor at Harvard Medical School and Director of the Behavioral Medicine Service at MGH, and led behavioral science studies at Fenway Health. He has been PI or protocol chair of 16 federally funded studies (via NIMH, NIDA, and NIAID) across two different clinical research areas: adult/adolescent ADHD, and health behavior change (HIV prevention and treatment). He has served as Editor of the journal *Cognitive and Behavioral Practice* and is currently an Associate Editor of *Journal of Consulting and Clinical Psychology*, and has published over 300 peer-reviewed scientific publications in his areas of research.